LOVE
LETTERS
OF KINGS
& QUEENS

LOVE
LETTERS
OF KINGS
& QUEENS

Edited by
DANIEL SMITH

greenfinch

First published in Great Britain in 2021 by

Greenfinch
An imprint of Quercus Editions Ltd
Carmelite House
50 Victoria Embankment
London EC4Y 0DZ

An Hachette UK company

A CIP catalogue record for this book is available
from the British Library

HB ISBN 978-1-52941-352-6
Ebook ISBN 978-1-52941-353-3

10 9 8 7 6 5 4 3 2 1

Typeset in Sabon and Requiem by seagulls.net
Cover design by Paileen Currie
Printed and bound in Great Britain by Clays Ltd, Elcograf S.p.A.

Papers used by Greenfinch are from well-managed forests
and other responsible sources.

For Rosie

Contents

Introduction

'I think the king is but a man, as I am. The violet
smells to him as it doth to me. The element shows to
him as it doth to me. All his senses have but human
conditions. His ceremonies laid by, in his nakedness
he appears but a man.'

King Henry in Shakespeare's *Henry V*

From ancient times, when monarchs secured their rule
through fear and the promise of protection, to the modern
era, when royalty often seems little more than the glitziest
manifestation of celebrity, it has always been difficult to
envisage rulers as being 'just like us'. Monarchs and rulers
have necessarily been apart from most of us. And let's be
clear, for most of history they have actively set themselves
apart. You don't get to live in a big castle, eat and imbibe
the finest food and drink available, wear the richest fabrics,
sport frankly ridiculous amounts of bling and get to tell
everybody else what to do unless you have worked very hard

3

to persuade other people that you deserve it more than they do. Quite a few of them down the years, let's remember, have been entirely convinced that it is God who put them on their thrones in the first place.

Yet, as King Henry acknowledges in the quotation above, even kings and queens, emperors and empresses are, ultimately, just people: human beings with talents and strengths but failings and foibles too; humans who sometimes rise to greatness and other times fall far short in the most basic measures of achievement; individuals who feel great love and affection and compassion along with hate and anger and disdain. They are people, in other words, who feel the full gamut of emotions and whose thoughts and actions are constantly subject to those emotions. Striking the balance between the natural feelings that we all experience and the peculiar demands of being a ruler is not an easy one. As the celebrated historian Robert K. Massie once said of Catherine the Great: 'The love of power and the power to attract love were not easy to reconcile.'

Where monarchy has traditionally promoted an image of superiority and 'apartness', most of the rest of us are in turn guilty of imposing a narrative on the lives of rulers. We expect certain things of them. When they are young, we cast them as beautiful princes and princesses destined for a fairytale 'happy ever after'. And when, as they almost always do, those same fabled princes and princesses grow up and somehow fall below our expectations, they are recast as disappointments, failures, pariahs. This is particularly true when it comes to their personal lives. So often, the fairy-tale is demanded even when we know that such stories have little basis in reality. As such, the love life of a royal person-age becomes performative in a way that many of us never need to worry about. The ups and downs that most of us accept as a natural part of our emotional lives become vastly amplified, so that the ups become magical moments for mass consumption and the downs evolve too often into sources of national, and even international, consternation. In the words of Wallis Simpson: 'You have no idea how hard it is to live out a great romance.'

The letters collected in this volume consistently reveal two truths. Firstly, that rulers from down through the ages experienced just the same kinds and depths of emotions – good and bad – as the rest of us. In other words, we'll discover that love (and, yes, lust), and their many variants and counterpoints, are universals that unite regardless of social status. But, secondly, love in the royal context has some peculiar aspects all of its own. In particular, we will witness how affairs of the heart may both guide and be guided by great affairs of state. We shall read, for instance, of numerous marriages founded on the needs of a nation rather than the heartfelt longings of an individual. Similarly, we'll see how the fates of nations were decided by the whim of a monarch's heart. How might things have been different, for instance, if Henry VIII had not been compelled to wed his brother's widow but had been allowed to marry for love instead? It is highly likely that Henry would then never have diverged from the rule of the Pope in order to secure a divorce, and that England (and then Britain) might have remained a Catholic country until the present day.

The hardest task with a collection such as this is to decide what to include and, equally, what to leave out. Alas, space constrictions prohibit using all of the magnificent material that I would have wanted. That said, it is also true that an anthologist is ultimately guided by what is available. In the case of royal love letters, a lot of them get lost in the mists of time but there is added impetus to hide and destroy them too. One suspects, for example, that Charles II, the 'Merry Monarch' with a reputation for prodigious lustiness, sent an awful lot of love missives over his lifetime. But equally, one is left to conclude, he was pretty careful to make sure he did not leave a vast paper trail of his indiscretions for posterity. On the other hand, we owe the existence of Henry VIII's extraordinary collection of letters to Anne Boleyn to whoever felt it pertinent to obtain them and deposit them in the Vatican archives – an individual, we may safely assume, who was not necessarily interested in looking out for the king's personal interests. But that collection also highlights another problem – very often, we can bear witness only to half of an amorous exchange simply because we have access only to one party's letters.

These obstacles and challenges aside, I have aimed to include correspondence that spans the centuries and which, in some way or another, shines a light on the usually unseen corners of royal romance. While most of the letters concern English and British monarchs, they inevitably encompass correspondents originating from many different parts of Europe. I have also chosen to include a snapshot of the love missives of two giants of European history, each of whom happened to bequeath us a particularly rich literary canon: Catherine the Great of Russia and Napoleon Bonaparte.

A note on language. The originals of the letters that follow were written in an array of languages. As well as English, there is French, German, Spanish and Russian. Some of the English monarchs were far more comfortable, for example, expressing themselves in courtly French or German than English. Moreover, the English of Queen Victoria is tonally very different to the English we are used to reading and hearing today. But go back further still, via Charles I and Henry VIII through to Edward II's reign in the early-fourteenth century, and the idioms can seem quite alien. Occasionally it has been necessary to amend spellings and the like to ensure each letter remains comprehensible to a contemporary reader. But at all times I have aimed to use translations and transcriptions that faithfully represent the spirit of the originals.

I am very grateful to Kathryn Warner – author of *Edward II: The Unconventional King* and *Isabella of France: The Rebel Queen* (both Amberley Publishing), as well as host of http:// edwardthesecond.blogspot.com – for permission to use her translation of the letter from Isabella of France to Henry II. Also to Douglas Smith – author of *Love & Conquest: Personal Correspondence of Catherine the Great and Prince Grigory Potemkin* (Northern Illinois University Press) – for permission to reproduce translations of some of the letters in his book. And finally, to the Institut Pasteur for generously allowing me to include letters between Edward VIII and Wallis Simpson, the latter having granted the institute the copyright on her literary estate.

I have attempted to put each set of correspondence into some historical context. The introductions are not intended to be exhaustive summaries of each ruler's reign, but rather they seek to overlay the evolution of their emotional lives on top of the major political forces at play upon them as royal figureheads. But it is the letters themselves that are the stars – the conduit into the hearts and souls of these kings and queens and their lovers and spouses. Here, then, are private messages between people in love – by turns tender, heartfelt and warm (and sporadically scandalous and outrageous too) – that simultaneously document the passions that changed the course of history.

Edward II and Isabella of France

Edward was born on 25 April 1284 at Caernarfon Castle in Wales, the son of King Edward I and Eleanor of Castile. The couple had at least fourteen children together but within a few months of Edward's birth, the last of his surviving three older brothers died, leaving him as the infant heir apparent.

From a young age, much thought was given to the marital prospects of the prince. When he was just six years old, he was promised to Margaret of Norway (herself then only seven), since she was considered to have a good claim to the Scottish throne. Sadly, though, she died of an unspecified illness on a trip from Norway to Scotland before the year was out. Attention then turned to France as the potential source of a future bride, but that plan was scuppered when war erupted between England and France in 1294. Philip IV of France then personally vetoed a potential union with a daughter of the Count of Flanders.

Edward's mother died in 1290 and the young teen prince ruled as England's regent while his father went off to defend his lands in Gascony in the late 1290s. The king eventually signed a peace treaty with Philip IV, which allowed for him to take the French king's sister, Margaret, as his second wife. Prince Edward, meanwhile, was pledged to marry Philip's infant daughter, Isabella, at an unspecified time in the future.

Fortunately, Prince Edward seems genuinely to have taken to Margaret and, in 1301, he was made Prince of Wales. He became king six years later on the death of his father and was immediately faced with an array of pressing problems – most significantly, growing dissatisfaction at English rule in the then kingless Scotland, along with strained relations with France over the English monarchy's claims on Gascony. Moreover, Edward I's military campaigns had drained the royal coffers so that his son inherited a Crown in severe debt, not to mention a class of barons disgruntled at having to provide evermore funding to the monarchy.

Edward commenced negotiations in earnest for his marriage to Isabella, hopeful that a union would secure his situation in Gascony and swell the royal purse too. Sure enough, he and Isabella were married in France on 25 January 1308. Among their wedding presents was a purported fragment of the True Cross from the bride's father, along with a hefty dowry. The couple travelled to England the following month, where their nuptials were lavishly celebrated at Westminster Abbey. But Isabella was still just twelve years old, and Edward twenty-four.

There can be little doubt that he was taking lovers elsewhere during this time. Edward had also developed a close relationship with a nobleman called Piers Gaveston, which infuriated many of his barons (the king left Gaveston in charge of his kingdom when he went to France to marry Isabella) and led at least some observers to speculate as to whether it was sexual in nature. Gaveston was ultimately seized by a band of barons and executed in 1312. That same year, Isabella gave birth to a son (who would become Edward III) and three more children followed over the next nine years.

Shortly after the birth of their first child, the king and queen travelled to Paris in a bid to smooth over relations with France. It was a largely successful mission and marked a high point in Edward's reign. But hard times were around the corner. In 1314, his army suffered a crippling defeat against the forces of Robert the Bruce at Bannockburn in Scotland. Meanwhile, a large number of his English barons continued to agitate, their dissatisfaction only aggravated by a series of famines. Tensions between the monarch and his barons finally spilled over into civil war in 1321. Edward managed to suppress the conflict, but at significant cost. Moreover, a year later Edward's brother-in-law, Charles, ascended to the French throne and relations between the countries faltered again. War broke out in 1324 and, in 1325, Isabella was sent to France in a bid to negotiate a new settlement.

The negotiations were far from easy and might have failed altogether were Isabella and Charles not brother and sister. Peace was secured, but only in return for Edward paying homage to the French king. Edward was wary of travelling to Gascony to do this in person so sent his eldest son instead. Now, Edward and Isabella's relationship took a turn for the worse. In truth, they had not been on good terms when she left for France. She had tired of the personal cost – to herself and to close friends – of her husband's various conflicts. She had also embarked on an affair with a lordly gentleman, Roger Mortimer. Rather than return home, Isabella set up base in Paris along with Mortimer. The pair and Isabella's son, Edward, now planned to launch an invasion against her husband, which they undertook in September 1325. By October, the king had been forced from London and within a few months he was besieged in Caerphilly Castle in Wales, many of his closest supporters having been rounded up and executed. By January 1327 Edward II faced a horrible dilemma – abdicate in favour of his son, or face being overthrown and his son disinherited in favour of another claimant to the throne entirely. Reluctantly, he chose the first option, with Isabella acting as regent on her son's behalf.

Edward died on 21 September 1327 in mysterious circumstances that have never been fully unravelled. Soon, Isabella and Mortimer's rule ran into its own problems, and in 1330 King Edward III had Mortimer arrested and executed. Among the charges against him was the murder of Edward II. Isabella, though, was spared by her son and lived out a comfortable retirement until her death in 1358.

The Letters

The following letters were written in 1325, when Isabella was in France negotiating a peace between her homeland and her husband's realm. The first note little suggests the drama that is about to proceed. Either Isabella has skillfully pulled the wool over her husband's eyes concerning her intentions, or else we must assume from her language ('My very sweet heart') that, at this stage, she remained committed to her marriage. The second letter, though, points clearly towards the troubles that lie ahead.

Letter 1:

Isabella to Edward (31 March 1325)

My very sweet heart, with the assent of your council I will remain in these parts as long as I have your permission, and with me remain the Bishop of Norwich and my cousin [the Earl] of Richmond. By the advice of the Pope's messages and of all of us, the Bishop of Winchester and Master William Airmyn will come to you to inform you more fully of the said affairs; and also by advice of the Pope's said messages and with the assent of my said brother, the Lord of Sully and the said Bishop of Orange will also come to you, and the Archbishop of Vienne will remain in the parts of Paris until you have written your wishes.

My very sweet heart, I beg you and request of you as humbly as I may, that you may please excuse me and the others who by your command are here with me that we did not write to you sooner that I had come to my said brother, but because of the uncertainty and inconstancy we have found, we could not write to you sooner with an exact record, and we did not dare to write of anything else until we had written to you on this matter. My very sweet heart, may the Holy Spirit by his grace save and protect you always. Written at Poissy the last day of March.

Letter 2:

Edward to Isabella (1 December 1325)

Lady – Oftentimes have we sent you, both before and after the homage, of our great desire to have you with us, and of our grief of heart at your long absence; and, as we understand that you do us great mischief by this, we will that you come to us with all speed, and without further excuses.

Before the homage was performed, you made the advancement of that business an excuse; and now that we have sent by the Honourable Father, the Bishop of

Winchester, our safe conduct to you, you will not come, for
the fear and doubt of Hugh le Despencer [a close friend
and advisor to Edward, whom Isabella detested]; whereat
we cannot marvel too much, when we recall your flattering
deportment towards each other in our presence, so amicable
and sweet was your deportment, with especial assurances
and looks, and other tokens of the firmest friendship; and
also, since then, your very especial letters to him of late date,
which he has shown to us.

And, certes, lady, we know for truth, and so know you,
that he has always procured from us all the honour he
could for you, nor to you hath either evil or villainy been
done since you entered into our companionship; unless,
peradventure, as you may yourself remember, once when
we had cause to give you secretly some words of reproof
for your pride, but without other harshness; and, doubtless,
both God and the law of our Holy Church require you to
honour us, and for nothing earthly to trespass against our
commandments or to forsake our company. And we are
much displeased how the homage has been made to our
dearest brother, the King of France, and we have such fair
prospect of amity, that you, whom we sent to make the peace,
should be the cause (which God forefend!) of increasing the
breach between us by things that are feigned and contrary
to the truth. Wherefore, we charge you as urgently as we can
that, ceasing from all pretences, delays and false excuses,

you come to us with all the haste you can. Our said bishop has reported to us that our brother, the King of France, told you in his presence, that, by your safe conduct, you would not be delayed, or molested, in coming to us as a wife should to her lord. And, as to your expenses, when it shall be that you will come to us as a wife should to her lord, we will provide that there shall be no deficiency in aught that is pertaining to you, and that you be not in any way dishonoured by us. Also we require of you that our dear son, Edward, return to us with all possible speed, for we much desire to see him, and to speak with him.

Henry VIII and His Six Wives

Henry Tudor was born on 28 June 1491 at Greenwich Palace (then some distance outside of London) to King Henry VII and Elizabeth of York. He was their third child and second son, his elder brother Arthur being the Prince of Wales and heir to the throne. Henry was created Duke of York and in 1501 attended the wedding of Arthur to Catherine of Aragon, daughter of the Spanish King Ferdinand II of Aragon and Queen Isabella I of Castile. Arthur and Catherine's union was one that Henry VII had enthusiastically pursued to ensure peace between the great nations.

But just a year later, the seemingly robust Arthur succumbed to illness and died. Henry, still only ten years old, was now heir and assumed a host of titles from his brother including Duke of Cornwall and Prince of Wales. But titles were not all that he inherited. In 1503 he was contracted to marry Catherine, his own brother's widow – a match he resisted for much of his teens. But after his father died in 1509, the new King Henry VIII, still just seventeen, seems to have had a change of heart and took Catherine as his queen in June that year. She was a little short of six years his senior.

Catherine soon fell pregnant but a daughter was stillborn in January 1510. A year later, she gave birth to a son, who was named Henry, but who died just a few weeks later. Two more stillbirths followed and the marriage strained under the couple's mutual sorrow, but then, in 1516, a healthy daughter arrived, whom they named Mary. Although Henry and Catherine's relationship improved with parenthood, Henry took on a series of mistresses. One, Elizabeth Blount, bore him an illegitimate son in 1519. Henry acknowledged the boy, Henry FitzRoy, and made him Duke of Richmond when he was six years old, leading to suspicions that, in the absence of a legitimate son, Henry might seek eventually to have the young duke succeed him as king.

As a young man, Henry was handsome, sporty and charismatic, but the absence of a legitimate son gnawed away at him, a missing part in the complete picture of kingship he wished to present. By the middle of the 1520s, he had virtually lost hope that Catherine would ever give him the male heir he dreamed of. Around this time, a young woman who served as maid of honour to his wife turned his head. Her name was Anne Boleyn. Henry already knew the family well, having earlier conducted an affair with Anne's older sister, Mary. Anne was at first reluctant to become his lover but Henry – now in his mid-thirties and running out of time to secure a male heir – decided that he must divorce Catherine and marry his new infatuation. His pursuit of this divorce in the face of papal opposition led to his momentous split with the Catholic Church.

After a union of twenty-four years, Henry cast Catherine aside, their marriage declared null and void. Henry and Anne participated in a secret marriage ceremony in late 1532 and then a second, public service in early 1533. All seemed well set for Anne when she quickly fell pregnant, although Henry's joy was tempered when she gave birth to a girl, Elizabeth. Gradually, Henry found that the independent spirit and lively intellect that had so attracted him to Anne in the first place now began to aggravate when she refused to be the passive, compliant spouse he expected. When Anne suffered a failed pregnancy in 1534, Henry took the absence of a male heir as further evidence that the marriage had run its course and began seeking advice as to how he might end it.

In 1536 the queen was pregnant once more, but when news arrived that Henry had been badly injured in a fall from his horse during a tournament, she miscarried. It proved a disappointment too far for their partnership. With Henry having already taken a new, younger lover – Jane Seymour – Anne found herself at the centre of allegations that spanned adultery, incest, conspiracy and witchcraft. She was arrested, convicted on evidence of dubious quality and sentenced to death. On 19 May 1536, in the grounds of the Tower of London, the vivacious Boleyn girl was beheaded.

Henry did not take long to move on. He became engaged to Jane Seymour the following day and the couple were married within the fortnight. In October the following year, Jane gave Henry the gift he had so longed for, a son, whom they named Edward. But there was to be a sting in the tail – Jane contracted an infection related to her labour and she was dead before the month was out.

The line of succession apparently secured, Henry next looked to take a wife who might be of strategic political value. He undertook this next project from a position of relative strength. He was on reasonable terms with the king of France, while the Catholic king of Spain and Holy Roman Emperor, Charles V, had so many calls on his time that interference in English affairs was relatively low down his list of concerns. Moreover, Henry had been greatly enriched by the dissolution of the monasteries that followed the break with the Vatican. However, he remained alert to the threat of a Catholic invasion, particularly when France and Spain grew closer in the late 1530s. He therefore alighted on the Duke of Cleves, a man who trod the religious middle ground between Catholicism and Lutheranism, as a potential ally. Henry agreed to marry the duke's daughter, Anne, encouraged in this endeavour by a portrait of his potential bride executed by the court painter Hans Holbein the Younger.

The pair met for the first time at the very start of 1540 and married within a week, but it was quickly apparent that there was nothing in the way of natural chemistry between them. Within a matter of months, Henry had had enough and pressed her for an annulment. She acceded and their marriage was formerly terminated in July 1540 on the grounds that it was unconsummated and that she had previously been betrothed to another. She did at least receive a healthy financial settlement and took the title of 'the king's sister'. Crucially, she also managed to stay at one with her head.

Almost instantly, Henry was married again. On 28 July 1540 he wedded Catherine Howard, a teenage beauty who had been a cousin of, and lady-in-waiting to, Anne Boleyn. He showered her with gifts of land and jewellery, his obsession with her shining brightly for a while. But it was not long before there were problems here, too. Specifically, word got to him that his young bride had previously been involved with her secretary, Francis Dereham, and that she was also engaged in an affair with a courtier, Thomas Culpeper. While the exact truth of these allegations remains disputed, the end result was that both men were executed, as was Catherine in February 1542.

Yet still Henry would not swear off marriage. He made vows for the final time in 1543, this time to Katherine Parr, who was herself embarking on a third marriage (her previous husbands having both died). She had come to the king's notice as part of the household of his eldest daughter, Mary, and they married at Hampton Court Palace. She played an important political role in the life of the nation, not least by persuading Henry that his previously excluded daughters, Mary and Elizabeth, should be returned to the line of succession after his son, Edward.

By now, Henry was severely overweight and burdened with an assortment of serious health complaints. He died in the Palace of Whitehall in London on 28 January 1547. His widow received a generous pension and went on to marry Thomas Seymour, a brother of Henry's previous wife, Jane. Henry was succeeded by his son Edward and, as events would play out, all his surviving children – son and daughters – would go on to hold the throne.

The Letters: Catherine of Aragon

Our first pair of letters comes from Henry's first wife. They start with a celebration of the decisive victory of the English army over the Scottish forces of James IV at Flodden in 1513. Henry was in France at the time and the first note reveals the queen's loyalty to him. The second letter is the last that Catherine ever wrote to the man who had once been her husband. Its tone is startlingly different to the first, but Catherine emerges from it as magnanimous, generous, caring and forgiving – rendering Henry's reported lack of grief upon her death all the more tragic.

Letter 1:

Catherine to Henry (16 September 1513)

Sir – My Lord Howard has sent me a letter open to Your
Grace, within one of mine, by the which you shall see at
length the great victory that our Lord has sent your subjects
in your absence; and for this cause it is no need herein to
trouble Your Grace with long writing, but, to my thinking,
this battle has been to Your Grace and all your realm the
greatest honour that could be, and more than you should
win at the Crown of France. Thanked be God of it: and I
am sure your Grace forgets not to do this, which shall be
cause to send you many more such great victories, as I trust
He shall do.

My husband, for hastiness, with Rogecrosse I could
not send Your Grace the piece of the King of Scots coat
that John Glyn now brings. In this Your Grace shall see
how I can keep my promise, sending you for your banners
a king's coat. I thought to send the king himself unto you,
but our Englishmen's hearts would not suffer it. It should
have been better for him to have been in peace than have
this reward. All that God sends is for the best. My Lord of
Surrey, my Henry, would fain know your pleasure in the
burying of the King of Scot's body, for he has written to me
so. With the next messenger Your Grace pleasure may be
herein known. And with this I make an end, praying God to
send you home shortly, for without this no joy here can be

accomplished – and for the same I pray, and now go to our Lady at Walsyngham that I promised so long ago to see.

At Woborne, the XVI day of September.

I send Your Grace herein a bill found in a Scottishman's purse of such things as the French king sent to the said King of Scots to make war against you, beseeching you to send Mathew hither as soon this messenger comes to bring me tidings from Your Grace.

Your humble wife and true servant,

Catherine

Letter 2:

Catherine to Henry (7 January 1536)

My most dear lord, king and husband,

The hour of my death now drawing on, the tender love I owe you forces me, my case being such, to commend myself to you, and to put you in remembrance with a few words of the health and safeguard of your soul, which you ought to prefer before all worldly matters, and before the care and pampering of your body, for the which you have cast me into many calamities and yourself into many troubles. For my part, I pardon you everything, and I wish to devoutly pray to God that He will pardon you also. For the rest, I commend unto you our daughter Mary, beseeching you to be a good father unto her, as I have heretofore desired. I entreat you also, on behalf of my maids, to give them marriage portions, which is not much, they being but three. For all my other servants I solicit the wages due them, and a year more, lest they be unprovided for. Lastly, I make this vow, that mine eyes desire you above all things.

Catherine the Queen

The Letters: Anne Boleyn

Now comes a series of letters between Henry VIII and Anne Boleyn. The first purports to be from Anne and would likely have been written between 1522 and 1527, thanking Henry for her appointment as maid of honour to his then wife, Catherine of Aragon. We cannot be sure of its authenticity though – while its whereabouts is unknown, it was first cited by the Italian historian Gregorio Leti in the seventeenth century, although some have cast doubt on his reliability. It should thus be treated with caution but provides intriguing reading nonetheless. Seventeen letters from Henry to Anne follow, written between 1527 and 1528 and later deposited in the Vatican archives (presumably by someone who considered there was value to be had from evidence of their affair). The final letter in this section is said to have been written from Anne to Henry as she awaited execution in the Tower of London. It was apparently discovered among the property of Thomas Cromwell, Henry's chief minister at the time of her execution. However, historians continue to argue as to whether it really is the work of Anne's hand.

Letter 1:

Anne to Henry (c. 1522–27)

Sire – It belongs only to a great king like yourself, to whom Nature has given a heart full of generosity towards the sex, to repay by such exceptional thanks a trivial and very brief conversation with a girl. Inexhaustible as is the treasury of Your Majesty's bounties, I beg you to consider that it cannot be sufficient for your generosity, since if the latter recompenses a brief conversation by so great a gift, what will your generosity be able to perform on behalf of those who are willing to swear an entire obedience to its wishes? However great may be the bounties that I have received, the joy that is mine of finding myself loved by a king whom I adore, and to whom I would with gladness sacrifice my heart, if fortune had rendered it worthy of being offered him, will be infinitely greater. The warrant of maid of honour to the queen with which you have honoured me, induces me to think that Your Majesty has some liking for me, since this will give me the means of seeing you more frequently and of assuring you with my own lips, which I shall do on the first opportunity, that I shall be always Your Majesty's very obliged and very obedient servant, without any reserve,

Anne Boleyn

Letter 2:

**Henry to Anne (sometime after May 1527, when Anne
had returned to her family home of Hever Castle)**

By turning over in my thoughts the contents of your last
letters, I have put myself into a great agony, not knowing
how to understand them, whether to my disadvantage as I
understood some others, or not; I beseech you now, with the
greatest earnestness, to let me know your whole intention
as to the love between us two. For I must of necessity obtain
this answer from you, having been above a whole year struck
with the dart of love, and not yet sure whether I shall fail,
or find a place in your heart and affection. This uncertainty
has hindered me of late from naming you my mistress, since
you only love me with an ordinary affection; but if you please
to do the duty of a true and loyal mistress, and to give up
yourself, body and heart, to me, who will be, as I have been,
your most loyal servant (if your rigour does not forbid me),
I promise you that not only the name shall be given you, but
also that I will take you for my mistress, casting off all others
that are in competition with you, out of my thoughts and
affection, and serving you only. I beg you to give an entire
answer to this my rude letter, that I may know on what
and how far I may depend. But, if it does not please you to
answer me in writing, let me know some place, where I may
have it by word of mouth, and I will go thither with all my
heart. No more for fear of tiring you.

Written by the hand of him, who would willingly remain yours,

H. Rex

This next letter was written between May and July 1527; the code at the end of this short note remains undeciphered.

Letter 3:

Henry to Anne

Though it does not belong to a gentleman to take his lady in the place of a servant, however, in following your desires, I willingly grant it, so that you may be more agreeable in the place that you yourself have chosen, than you have been in that which I gave you. I shall be heartily obliged to you, if you please to have some remembrance of me. 6. N. R. i. de R. O. M. V. E. Z.

Henry Rex

Letter 4:

Henry to Anne (sometime between May and July 1527)

Although, my mistress, you have not been pleased to remember the promise that you made me when I was last with you, which was that I should hear news of you, and have an answer to my last letter; yet I think it belongs to a true servant (since otherwise he can know nothing) to send to enquire of his mistress's health; and, for to acquit myself of the office of a true servant, I send you this letter begging you to give me an account of the state you are in, which I pray God may continue as long in prosperity, as I with my own; and, that you may the oftener remember me, I send you by this bearer, a buck killed late last night by my hand, hoping, when you eat of it, you will think on the hunter; and thus for want of more room I will make an end of my letter.

Written by the hand of your servant, who often wishes you in your brother's room,

H. Rex

Letter 5:
Henry to Anne (sometime between May and July 1527)

My mistress and friend – I and my heart put ourselves in your hands, begging you to recommend us to your favour, and not to let absence lessen your affection to us. For it were a great pity to increase our pain, which absence alone does sufficiently, and more than I could ever have thought; bringing to my mind a point of astronomy, which is that the farther the Moors are from us, the farther too is the sun, and yet his heat is the more scorching; so it is with our love, we are at a distance from one another, and yet it keeps its fervency, at least on my side. I hope the like on your part, assuring you that the uneasiness of absence is already too severe for me; and when I think of the continuance of that which I must of necessity suffer, it would seem intolerable to me, were it not for the firm hope I have of your unchangeable affection for me; and now, to put you sometimes in mind of it, and seeing I cannot be present in person with you, I send you the nearest thing to that possible, that is, my picture set in bracelets, with the whole device, which you know already, wishing myself in their place, when it shall please you.

This from the hand of your servant and friend,

H. Rex

A short time before this next letter was written, Anne had gifted Henry a piece of jewellery in response to his recent proposal of marriage.

Letter 6:

Henry to Anne (July 1527)

For a present so valuable that nothing could be more (considering the whole of it) I return you my most hearty thanks, not only on account of the costly diamond, and the ship in which the solitary damsel is tossed about; but chiefly for the fine interpretation and too humble submission that your goodness hath made to me. For I think it would be very difficult for me to find an occasion to deserve it, if I was not afflicted by your great humanity and favour, which I have sought, do seek, and will always seek to preserve by all the services in my power; and this is my firm intention and hope, according to the motto, *Aut illic aut nullibi* [either here or nowhere]. The demonstrations of your affections are such, the fine thoughts of your letter so cordially expressed that they oblige me for ever to honour, love and serve you sincerely, beseeching you to continue in the same firm and constant purpose; and assuring you, that, on my part, I will not only make you a suitable return, but out-do you in loyalty of heart if it be possible. I desire you also, that, if at any time before this I have in any sort offended you, you would give me the same absolution that you ask, assuring you that hereafter my heart shall be dedicated to you alone, I with my body was so too, God can do it, if He pleases; to whom I pray once a day for that end; hoping that at length my prayers will be heard. I wish the time may be short, but I shall think it long, till we shall see one another.

Written by the hand of the secretary, who in heart, body and will, is your loyal and most assured servant,

H. no other (AB) seeks Rex

Letter 7:
Henry to Anne (July 1527)

To my mistress – Because the time seems to me very long since I have heard from you, or concerning your health; the great affection I have for you has obliged me to send this bearer to be better informed, both of your health and pleasure, particularly because, since my last parting with you,

I have been told, that you have entirely changed the opinion
in which I left you, and that you would neither come to court
with your mother, nor any other way; which report, if true, I
cannot wonder enough at, being persuaded in my own mind,
that I have never committed any offence against you; and it
seems a very small return for the great love I bear you, to be
kept at a distance from the person and presence of a woman
in the world that I value most; and, if you love me with as
much affection as I hope you do, I am sure, the distance of
our two persons would be a little uneasy to you. Though
this does not belong so much to the mistress as the servant.
Consider well, my mistress, how greatly your absence grieves
me; I hope it is not your will that it should be so; but, if I
heard for certain, that you yourself desired it, I could do no
other than complain of my ill fortune, and by degrees abate
my great folly; and so, for want of time, I make an end of my
rude letter, desiring you to give credit to this bearer in all he
will tell you from me.

Written by the hand of your entire servant.

Letter 8:

Henry to Anne (February 1528)

Darling – These shall be only to advertise you that this bearer
and his fellow be despatched with as many things to compass
our matter, and to bring it to pass as our wits could imagine
or devise, which brought to pass, as I trust by their diligence,

it shall be shortly, you and I shall have our desired end. This should be more to my heart's ease, and more quietness to my mind, than any other thing in this world, as with God's grace shortly I trust shall be proved, but not so soon as I would it were; yet I will assure you there shall be no time lost that may be won, and further cannot be done, for *ultra posse non est esse* [one cannot do more than is possible]. Keep him not too long with you, but desire him for your sake to make the more speed; for the sooner we shall have word from him, the sooner shall our matter come to pass; and thus, upon trust of your short repair to London, I make an end of my letter, mine own sweetheart.

Written with the hand of him which desires as much to be yours, as you do to have him,

H. R.

Letter 9:

Henry to Anne (16 June 1528)

There came to me in the night the most afflicting news possible. For I have reason to grieve upon three accounts. First, because I heard of the sickness of my mistress [Anne was suffering with sweating sickness], whom I esteem more than all the world, whose health I desire as much as my own, and the half of whose sickness I would willingly bear to have her cured. Secondly, because I fear I shall suffer yet longer that tedious absence that has hitherto given me all possible uneasiness, and, as far as I can judge, is like to give me more.

I pray God He would deliver me from so troublesome a tormentor. The third reason is, because the physician, in whom I trust most, is absent at present, when he could do me the greatest pleasure. For I should hope by him, and his means, to obtain one of my principle joys in this world, that is, my mistress cured; however, in default of him, I send you the second, and the only one left, praying God that he may soon make you well, and then I shall love him more than ever. I beseech you to be governed by his advices with relation to your illness; by your doing which, I hope shortly to see you again, which will be to me a greater cordial than all the precious stones in the world.

Written by the secretary who is, and always will be, your loyal and most assured servant,

H. (AB) R.

Letter 10:

Henry to Anne (20 June 1528)

The uneasiness, my doubts about your health gave me, disturbed and frightened me extremely, and I should not have had any quiet without hearing a certain account. But now since you have felt nothing, I hope it is with you as with us; for when we were at Walton, two ushers, two valets de chambre, and your brother, master-treasurer, fell ill, and are now quite well; and since we have returned to your house at Hondson, we have been perfectly well, God be praised, and have not, at present, one sick person in the family; and, I think, if you would retire from the Surrey side, as we did, you would escape all danger. There is another thing that may comfort you, which is, that in truth in this distemper few or no women have been taken ill, and besides, no person of our court, and few elsewhere have died of it. For which reasons I beg of you, my entirely beloved, not to frighten yourself, nor to be too uneasy at our absence. For, wherever I am, I am yours, and yet we must sometimes submit to our misfortunes, for, whoever will struggle against fate, is generally but so much the farther from gaining his end; wherefore, comfort yourself, and take courage, and make this misfortune as easy to you as you can, and I hope shortly to make you sing for joy of your recall. No more at present for lack of time, but that I wish you in my arms, that I might a little dispel your unreasonable thoughts.

Written by the hand of him, who is, and always will be yours,

My, H. Rex, Lovely

Letter 11:

Henry to Anne (22 June 1528)

The cause of my writing at this time (good sweetheart) is only to understand of your good health and prosperity, whereof to know I would be as glad in manner my own, praying God, that and it be His pleasure, to send us shortly together, for I promise you I long for it, howbeit, trust it shall not be long too; and seeing my darling is absent, I can no less do, than to send her some flesh representing my name, which is hart's flesh for Henry, prognosticating, that hereafter, God willing ... which if he pleased I would were now ... No more to you at this time, mine own darling, but that with a wish I would we were together one evening with the hand of your,

H. R.

Letter 12:

Henry to Anne (written July 1528)

Since your last letters, my own darling, Walter Welche, Master Brown, John Carre, Yrion of Brearton, John Cocke, the apothecary, be fallen of the sweat in this house, and thanked be God all well recovered, so that as yet the plague is not fully ceased here; but I trust shortly it shall by the mercy of God; the rest of us yet be well, and I trust shall pass it, either not to have it, or at least as easily as the rest have done. As touching the matter of Wylton, my Lord Cardinal hath had the nuns before him, and examined them, Master Bell being present, which hath certified me that for a truth, that she hath confessed herself (which we would have had abbess) to have had two children by two sundry priests; and, further, since hath been kept by a servant of the Lord Broke, that was, and that not long ago. [Isabella Jordan, the abbess in question, was the subject of assorted accusations as to her

character. More pertinently, she had been appointed against
the wishes of Anne, who had hoped that one of her relatives
through marriage would fill the post. Henry is obviously
keeping a close eye on the affair on her behalf.] Wherefore
I would not for all the world clog your conscience nor mine
to make her ruler of a house that is of so ungodly demeanour;
nor I trust you would not, that neither for brother nor sister I
should so destain mine honour or conscience; and as touching
the prioress, or Dame Ellenor's eldest sister, though there is
not any evident case proved against them, and that the prioress
is so old, that of many years she could not be as she was named;
yet notwithstanding, to do you pleasure, I have done that
neither of them shall have it, but that some other and good
and well disposed woman shall have it; whereby the house shall
be the better reformed (whereof, I ensure you, it had much
need) and God much the better served.

As touching your abode at Hever, do therein as best shall
you like; for you know best what ere doth best for you; but I
would it were come thereto (if it pleased God) that neither
of us need care for that, for I ensure you I think it long. Such
is fallen sick of the sweats, and therefore I send you this
bearer, because I think you long to hear tidings from us, as
we do in likewise from you.

Writing with the hand, *de votre seul* (of yours only),

H. R.

Letter 13:

Henry to Anne (20 July 1528)

The approach of the time, which I have so long expected, rejoices me so much, that it seems almost ready come. However, the entire accomplishment cannot be till the two persons meet, which meeting is more desired by me than anything in this world; for what joy can be greater upon Earth, than to have the company of her who is my dearest friend? Knowing likewise that she does the same on her part, the thinking on which gives great pleasure. You may judge what an effect the presence of that person must have on me, whose absence has made a greater wound in my heart than either words or writing can express, and which nothing can cure, but her return; I beg you, dear mistress, to tell your father from me, that I desire him to hasten the appointment by two days, that he may be in court before the old term, or at farthest on the day prefixed; for otherwise I shall think, he will not do the lover's turn, as he said he would, nor answer my expectation. No more at present, for want of time; hoping shortly that by word of mouth I shall tell you the rest of my sufferings from your absence.

Written by the hand of the secretary, who wishes himself at present privately with you, and who is, and always will be, your royal and most assured servant,

H. no other (AB) seeks Rex

Letter 14:

Henry to Anne (21 July 1528)

Darling – I heartily recommend me to you, ascertaining you, that I am a little perplexed with such things as your brother shall on my part declare unto you, to whom I pray you give full credence, for it were too long to write. In my last letters I wrote to you that I trusted shortly to see you, which is better known at London than with any that is about me, whereof I not a little marvel but lack of discreet handling must needs be the cause thereof. No more to you at this time, but that I trust shortly, our meeting shall not depend upon other men's light handlings but upon your own.

Written with the hand of him that longs to be yours,

H. R.

Letter 15:

Henry to Anne (August 1528)

My own sweetheart – This shall be to advertise you of the great elengeness [misery, tedium] that I find here since your departing, for I assure you, methinketh the time longer since your departing now last than I was wont to do a whole fortnight; I think your kindness and my fervency of love causeth it, for otherwise I would not thought it possible, that for so little a while it should have grieved me, but now that I am coming towards you, methinketh my pains been half released, and also I am right well comforted, insomuch that my book maketh substantially for my matter, in writing whereof I have spent above four hours this day, which caused me now to write the shorter letter to you at this time, because of same pain in my head, wishing myself (especially an evening) in my sweetheart's arms whose pretty duckys [that is to say, breasts] I trust shortly to kiss.

Written with the hand of him that was, is, and shall be yours by his will,

H. R.

Letter 16:

Henry to Anne (August 1528)

Darling – Though I have scant leisure, yet, remembering my promise, I thought it convenient to certify you briefly, in what case our affairs stand. As touching a lodging for you, we have got one, by my Lord Cardinal's means, the like whereof could not have been found hereabouts for all causes, as this bearer shall more show you. As touching our other affairs [Henry's desire to end his marriage to Catherine of Aragon], I ensure you there can be no more done, or more diligence used, nor all manners of dangers better both foreseen and provided for, so that I trust it shall be hereafter to both our comforts, the specialities whereof were both too long to be written, and hardly by messenger to be declared. Wherefore till you repair hither, I keep something in store, trusting it shall not be long to. For I have caused my lord, your father, to make his provisions with speed. And thus, for

lack of time, darling, I make an end of my letter, writing with
the hand of him, which I would were yours,

H. R.

Letter 17:

Henry to Anne (16 September 1528)

The reasonable request of your last letter, with the pleasure
I also take to know them, causes me to send you now this
news. The legat, which we most desire, arrived at Paris on
Sunday or Monday last past; so that I trust, by the next
Monday, to hear of his arrival at Calais: and then, I trust,
within a while after, to enjoy that which I have so longed
for, to God's pleasure, and both our comforts. No more, to
you at this present, my own darling, for lack of time; but
that I would you were in my arms, or I in yours; for I think
it is a long time since I kissed you.

Written after the killing of a hart, at eleven of the
clock; minding with God's grace tomorrow, mightily timely
to kill another, by the hand of him, which I trust shortly
shall be yours,

Henry R.

Letter 18:

Henry to Anne (late October 1528)

To inform you what joy it is to me to understand of your
conformableness with reason, and of the suppressing of

your useless and vain thoughts and fantasies with the bridle of reason, I assure you all the good of this world could not counterpoise for my satisfaction the knowledge and certainty thereof; wherefore, good sweetheart, continue the same not only in this, but in all your doings hereafter, for thereby shall come both to you and me the greatest quietness that may be in this world. The cause why this bearer stays so long, is the business that I have had to dress up gear for you, which I trust ere long to see you occupy, and then I trust to occupy yours, which shall be recompense to me for all my pains and labours. The unfeigned sickness of this well-willing legate somewhat retards his access to your person, but I trust verily, when God shall send him to health, he will with diligence recompense his demure, for I know well where he hath said (lamenting the reports that he shall be thought imperial) that it shall be well known in this matter, that he is not imperial. And this for lack of time, farewell.

Written with the hand which willingly would be yours, and so is the heart,

H. R.

Letter 19:

Anne to Henry (6 May 1536, Tower of London)

Sir – Your Grace's displeasure, and my imprisonment, are things so strange unto me, as what to write, or what to excuse, I am altogether ignorant. Whereas you send unto me (willing me to confess a truth, and so obtain your favour) by such a one whom you know to be mine ancient professed enemy; I no sooner received this message by him, than I rightly conceived your meaning; and if, as you say, confessing a truth indeed may procure my safety, I shall with all willingness and duty perform your command.

But let not Your Grace ever imagine that your poor wife will ever be brought to acknowledge a fault, where not so much as a thought thereof preceded. And to speak a truth, never prince had wife more loyal in all duty, and in all true affection, than you have ever found in Anne Boleyn, with which name and place I could willingly have contented myself, if God and Your Grace's pleasure had been so pleased. Neither did I at any time so far forget myself in my exaltation, or received queenship, but that I always looked for such an alteration as now I find; for the ground of my preferment being on no surer foundation than your Grace's fancy, the least alteration, I knew, was fit and sufficient to draw that fancy to some other subject. You have chosen me from a low estate to be your queen and companion, far beyond my desert or desire. If then, you found me worthy of such honour, good Your Grace let not any light fancy, or bad counsel of mine enemies, withdraw your princely favour from me; neither let that stain, that unworthy stain of a disloyal heart, towards your good Grace, ever cast so foul a blot on your most dutiful wife, and the infant princess, your daughter; try me, good king, but let me have a lawful trial,

and let not my sworn enemies sit as my accusers and judges;
yea, let me receive an open trial, for my truth shall fear no
open shame; then shall you see, either mine innocence cleared,
your suspicion and conscience satisfied, the ignominy and
slander of the world stopped, or my guilt openly declared. So
that, whatsoever God or you may determine of me, Your Grace
may be freed from an open censure; and mine offence being
so lawfully proved, Your Grace is at liberty, both before God
and man, not only to execute worthy punishment on me as
an unlawful wife, but to follow your affection already settled
on that party, for whose sake I am now as I am, whose name
I could some good while since have pointed unto; Your Grace
being not ignorant of my suspicion therein.

But, if you have already determined of me, and that not
only my death, but an infamous slander must bring you the
enjoying of your desired happiness; then I desire of God,
that He will pardon your great sin therein, and likewise mine
enemies, the instruments thereof; and that He will not call
you to a strict account for your unprincely and cruel usage
of me, at His general judgement seat, where both you and
myself must shortly appear, and in whose judgement, I doubt
not (whatsoever the world may think of me), my innocence
shall be openly known, and sufficiently cleared.

My last and only request shall be, that myself may only
bear the burden of Your Grace's displeasure, and that it may
not touch the innocent souls of those poor gentlemen, who,

as I understand, are likewise in strait imprisonment for my sake. If ever I have found favour in your sight; if ever the name of Anne Boleyn hath been pleasing in your ears, then let me obtain this request, and I will so leave to trouble Your Grace any further, with my earnest prayers to the Trinity to have Your Grace in His good keeping, and to direct you in all your actions.

From my doleful prison in the Tower, this 6th of May. – Your most loyal and ever faithful wife,

Anne Boleyn

The Letters: Jane Seymour

This next letter is a missive composed by Henry while his wife, Anne Boleyn, resided in the Tower of London facing death. Given that the king would become engaged to Jane within a day of Anne's execution, he can hardly be surprised that the pair were the subjects of a 'ballad … of great derision'.

Letter 1:
Henry to Jane (c. 14–19 May 1536)
My dear friend and mistress – The bearer of these few lines from your entirely devoted servant will deliver into your fair hands a token of my true affection for you, hoping you will keep it forever in your sincere love for me. Advertising you

that there is a ballad made lately of great derision against us, which if it goes much abroad and is seen by you, I pray you to pay no manner of regard to it. I am not at present informed who is the setter forth of this malignant writing but if he is found he shall be severely punished for it. For the things you lacked I have minded my lord to supply them to you as soon as he can buy them. This hoping shortly to receive you in these arms, I end for the present.

Your own servant and sovereign,

H. R.

The Letters: Anne of Cleves

Given the entire lack of spark between Henry and his fourth wife, Anne of Cleves, it is hardly a shock that there is no great collection of love missives as there is for Anne Boleyn. However, there is the extraordinary letter below that Anne sent in response to Henry's request for an annulment of their marriage in 1540. Anne's willingness to accept it with scarcely a complaint likely saved her life.

Letter 1:
Anne to Henry (11 July 1540)

Pleaseth your most excellent Majesty to understand that, whereas, at sundry times heretofore, I have been informed

and perceived, by certain lords and others of Your Grace's
council, of the doubts and questions that have been moved
and found in our marriage; and how hath petition thereupon
been made to Your Highness by your nobles and commons,
that the same might be examined and determined by the
holy clergy of this realm; to testify to Your Highness by my
writing, that which I have before promised by my word and
will, that is to say, that the matter should be examined and
determined by the said clergy, it may please Your Majesty
to know that, though this case must needs be most hard
and sorrowful unto me, for the great love that I bear to
your most noble person, having more regard to God and
His truth than to any worldly affection, as it beseemed
me, at the beginning, to submit me to such examination
and determination of the said clergy, whom I have and do
accept for judges competent in that behalf. So now being
ascertained how the same clergy hath therein given their
judgement and sentence, I knowledge myself hereby to
accept and approve the same wholly and entirely putting
myself, for my state and condition, to your Highness'
goodness and pleasure; most humbly beseeching Your
Majesty that, though it be determined that the pretended
matrimony between us is void and of none effect, whereby
I neither can nor will repute myself for Your Grace's wife,
considering this sentence (whereunto I stand) and Your
Majesty's clean and pure living with me, yet it will please

you to take me for one of your most humble servants, and so to determine of me, as I may sometimes have the fruition of your most noble presence; which as I shall esteem for a great benefit, so, my lords and other of Your Majesty's council, now being with me, have put me in comfort thereof; and that Your Highness will take me for your sister; for the which I most humbly thank you accordingly.

Thus, most gracious Prince, I beseech our Lord God to send your Majesty long life and good health, to God's glory, your own honour, and the wealth of this noble realm.

From Richmond, the 11th day of July, the 32nd year of Your Majesty's most noble reign.

Your Majesty's most humble sister and servant,

Anne (the daughter of Cleves)

The Letters: Catherine Howard

Overlapping with Anne of Cleves and next to marry the king came the ill-starred Catherine Howard. The first of her letters here is to Thomas Culpeper, the man with whom she was accused of having an affair while married to Henry – a claim that cost them both their lives. It has been suggested that rather than a love letter, this note may actually be read as Catherine's attempt to ingratiate herself with an individual threatening blackmail about her sexual past. We may never know for sure. The second letter is one she sent to Henry, confessing her various apparent crimes. Prior to its composition, she had been extensively questioned by Archbishop Cranmer about the various charges against her. He may well have persuaded her that such a confession might secure the king's mercy – which, of course, it did not.

Letter 1:

Catherine to Thomas Culpeper (c. July or August 1540)

Master Culpeper,

I heartily recommend me unto you, praying you to send me word how that you do. It was showed me that you were sick, the which thing troubled me very much till such time that I hear from you, praying you to send me word how that you do, for I never longed so much for a thing as I do to see you and to speak with you, the which I trust shall be shortly now.

That which comforts me very much when I think of it, and when I think again that you shall depart from me again, it makes my heart die to think what fortune I have that I cannot be always in your company.

Yet my trust is always in you that you will be as you have promised me, and in that hope I trust upon still, praying that you will come when my Lady Rochford is here, for then I shall be best at leisure to be at your commandment, thanking you for that you have promised me to be so good unto that poor fellow my man, which is one of the griefs that I do feel to depart from him for then I do know no one that I dare trust to send to you, and therefore I pray you take him to be with you that I may sometime hear from you one thing.

I pray you to give me a horse for my man, for I had much ado to get one and therefore I pray send me one by him and in so doing I am as I said before, and thus I take my leave of you, trusting to see you shortly again and I would you were with me now that you might see what pain I take in writing to you.

Yours as long as life endures,

Catherine

Letter 2:

Catherine to Henry (7 November 1541)

I, Your Grace's most sorrowful subject and most vile wretch in the world, not worthy to make any recommendation unto your most excellent Majesty, do only make my most humble submission and confession of my faults. And where no cause of mercy is given on my part, yet of your most accustomed mercy extended unto all other men undeserved, most humbly on my hands and knees do desire one particle thereof to be extended unto me, although of all other creatures I am most unworthy either to be called your wife or subject.

My sorrow I can by no writing express, nevertheless I trust your most benign nature will have some respect unto

my youth, my ignorance, my frailness, my humble confession
of my faults, and plain declaration of the same, referring
me wholly unto Your Grace's pity and mercy. First, at the
flattering and fair persuasions of Manox [Henry Manox,
her former music tutor and purported lover], being but
a young girl, I suffered him a sundry times to handle and
touch the secret parts of my body, which neither became me
with honesty to permit, nor him to require. Also, Francis
Dereham by many persuasions procured me to his vicious
purpose, and obtained first to lie upon my bed with his
doublet and hose, and after within the bed, and finally he
lay with me naked, and used me in such sort as a man uses
his wife, many and sundry times, and our company ended
almost a year before the king's Majesty was married to my
lady Anne of Cleves and continued not past one quarter of a
year, or a little above.

Now the whole truth being declared unto Your Majesty,
I most humbly beseech you to consider the subtle
persuasions of young men and the ignorance and frailness
of young women. I was so desirous to be taken unto Your
Grace's favour, and so blinded by the desire of worldly glory
that I could not, nor had grace to consider how great a
fault it was to conceal my former faults from Your Majesty,
considering that I intended ever during my life to be
faithful and true unto Your Majesty ever after. Nevertheless,
the sorrow of my offences was ever before my eyes,

considering the infinite goodness of Your Majesty towards
me from time to time ever increasing and not diminishing.
Now, I refer the judgement of my offenses with my life and
death wholly unto your most benign and merciful Grace,
to be considered by no justice of Your Majesty's laws but
only by your infinite goodness, pity, compassion and mercy,
without which I acknowledge myself worthy of the most
extreme punishment.

The Letters: Katherine Parr

*Of all his brides, Katherine Parr could justifiably claim to
have had the most worldly experience by the time she married
Henry. The first three letters here were written in 1544 when
the king was engaged in military endeavours against both the
Scots and French. Katherine offers him determined encouragement and support, and while these notes lack the passion
of some of the other letters in this chapter, they speak of a
perhaps more stable relationship between two individuals at
a later stage of life. The third is a fragment from Henry to
Katherine that survived a fire in Westminster in 1731, its sign-
off suggesting a sincere, if not overly excitable, regard for his
wife. Given the fates of her predecessors, this was doubtless a
comfortable place to be.*

Letter 1:

Katherine to Henry (July 1544)

... Although the distance of time and account of days
neither is long nor many Your Majesty's absence, yet the
want of your presence, so much desired and beloved by me,
maketh me that I cannot quietly pleasure in anything until
I hear from Your Majesty. The time, therefore, seemeth
to me very long, with a great desire to know how your
highness hath done since your departing hence, whose
prosperity and health I prefer and desire more than mine
own. And whereas I know Your Majesty's absence is never
without great need, yet love and affection compel me to
desire your presence.

Again, the same zeal and affection forces me to be
best content with that which is your will and pleasure.
Thus love maketh me in all things to set apart mine own
convenience and pleasure, and to embrace most joyfully
his will and pleasure whom I love. God, the knower of
secrets, can judge these words not to be written only with
ink, but most truly impressed on the heart. Much more I
omit, lest it be thought I go about to praise myself, or crave
a thank; which thing to do I mind nothing less, but a plain,
simple relation of the love and zeal I bear Your Majesty,
proceeding from the abundance of the heart. Wherein I
must confess I desire no commendation, having such just
occasion to do the same.

I make like account with Your Majesty as I do with God for his benefits and gifts heaped upon me daily, acknowledging myself a great debtor to him, not being able to recompense the least of his benefits; in which state I am certain and sure to die, yet I hope in His gracious acceptation of my good will. Even such confidence have I in Your Majesty's gentleness, knowing myself never to have done my duty as were requisite and meet for such a noble prince, at whose hands I have found and received so much love and goodness, that with words I cannot express it. Lest I should be too tedious to Your Majesty, I finish this, my scribbled letter, committing you to the governance of the Lord a long and prosperous life here, and after this life to enjoy the kingdom of His elect.

From Greenwich, by Your Majesty's humble and obedient servant, Katherine the Queen.

Letter 2:
Katherine to Henry (31 July 1544)
Pleaseth it Your Majesty to be advertised, this afternoon were brought unto me letters from Your Majesty's lieutenant of the north, declaring the apprehension of a Scottish ship by certain fishermen of Rye, and in the same certain Frenchmen and Scots, being sent with diverse letters and credence towards the French king and others in France. And because I thought this taking of them, with the interception

of the said letters, to be of much importance for the advancement of Your Majesty's affairs, ordained (I doubt not) of God, as well to the intent Your Highness might thereby certainly understand the crafty dealing and juggling of that nation, as also meet with the same after such sort as to your high wisdom shall be thought most convenient; I have presently sent such of the said letters as, upon the view of the same, appeared of most importance unto Your Majesty. There are a great number of other letters to the French king and others, both from the dowager and others, but they are either of the same effect that these be which I have sent unto Your Majesty, or general letters only for credence. My lords of Your Majesty's council have sent to have certain of the chief, both of the Scots and Frenchmen, sent up, upon whose examination your Majesty shall be farther advertised with diligence.

My Lord Prince and the rest of Your Majesty's children are all, thanks be to God, in very good health. And thus with my most humble commendations unto Your Majesty I pray Almighty God have the same in His most blessed keeping.

From Your Majesty's honour of Hampton Court, the last day of July, the 36th year of Your Majesty's most noble reign.

Your Grace's most humble, loving wife and servant,

Katherine the Queen, K. P.

Letter 3:

Katherine to Henry (25 August 1544)

Pleaseth it Your Majesty to be advertised, albeit I had at this present none occurrents of importance to be signified unto Your Highness, your realm being, thanks be to Almighty God, in very good order and quiet; yet, forasmuch as Richard Higham is at this time dispatched hence unto Your Majesty with a mass of 30,000l. [pounds], I thought it my duty to advertise Your Majesty of the sending of the same; praying Almighty God to send Your Majesty continuance of health and most prosperous success in all your Highness' most noble enterprises. My Lord Prince and the rest of Your Majesty's children be in very good health. And thus, with my most humble commendations unto Your Majesty, I pray Almighty God have the same in His most blessed keeping.

From Your Majesty's honour of Hampton Court, the 25th of August, the 36th year of your Majesty's most noble reign. Your Majesty's most humble, loving wife and servant,

Katherine the Queen, K. P.

Letter 4:

Henry to Katherine (8 September 1544)

... the castle afore named ... is at our commandment ... not likely to be recovered by the French men again, as we trust: not doubting with God's grace but that the castle and town shall shortly follow the same trade ... No more to you at this time sweetheart both for lack of time and great occupation of business, saving we pray you to give in our name our heart blessings to all our children, and recommendations to our cousin Margaret, and the rest of the ladies and gentlewomen, and to our Consell also.

Written with the hand of your loving husband,

Henry R.

Mary I and Philip II of Spain

Mary Tudor was born on 18 February 1516 at Greenwich Palace, the daughter of Henry VIII and his first wife, Catherine of Aragon. The only one of their children to survive infancy, she was raised a Roman Catholic and received tutoring in a range of disciplines considered suitable for a young princess, among them music, languages and dancing. Henry also groomed her for her potential future life as a ruler, for instance sending her to oversee the affairs of the powerful Council of Wales and the Marches when she was only ten.

Furthermore, the king kept a close eye on suitable candidates to eventually marry his daughter. While Mary was still a toddler, a union was negotiated with Francis, the infant son of the French king, Francis I, although the agreement was set aside after only a few years. In 1522, Charles V, the Holy Roman Emperor and a nephew of Mary's mother, replaced the young Francis as groom-in-the-making. This pact also fell away, however, and Mary was next offered up as a wife for either the, by then widowed, Francis I or one of his sons,

Henry, Duke of Orleans. These plans, though, faltered after England and France came to an accord without the need for a marriage, and so James V of Scotland came into the picture for a while.

What impacted most on Mary's life as she entered womanhood, was the state of her parents' own marriage. Henry, as we have seen, was intent on divorcing Catherine of Aragon, claiming that the scriptures forbade a union with his brother's wife. (Catherine for her part denied her marriage to Henry's brother, Arthur, was ever consummated, thus making it invalid.) Pope Clement VII was having none of Henry's argument – a position actively encouraged by the Catholic Charles V – and so the king opted instead to break with papal authority and have the marriage annulled by his own church officials. Catherine's time as queen was over and she was redesignated Dowager Princess of Wales. Mary, meanwhile, was declared illegitimate, sent away from court and forbidden to make contact with her mother. When Henry's new wife, Anne Boleyn, subsequently gave birth to a daughter, Elizabeth, this newborn became heir to the throne. Infuriated, Mary did not talk to her father for several years.

In 1536 Anne Boleyn was executed, at which time Elizabeth joined her half-sister in being removed from the line of succession and declared illegitimate. Then Henry married Jane Seymour, who encouraged rapprochement between the king and his daughters. Mary, with some reluctance, acknowledged Henry as head of the national Church free from papal influence, and also accepted her own illegitimacy. In return, she was welcomed back at court and received additional finances to live in the fashion that a princess might then expect to enjoy.

As she entered her mid-twenties, still unmarried, renewed attention was given to potential matches. Philip, Duke of Bavaria was considered a possible candidate but the issue of his Protestantism was too much for her to overcome. Then negotiations began for a marriage to the Duke of Cleves, but in the end it was her father who would marry the duke's sister instead. When Henry's chief minister, Thomas Cromwell, fell from favour, he was hit with the unlikely charge that he had plotted to marry Mary himself. Regardless, she remained unmarried.

By 1544, Henry was on to his last marriage and signed into law the Act of Succession that put both Mary and Elizabeth back in line for the throne. When Henry died three years later, it was the nine-year-old Edward, his son by Jane Seymour, who was crowned, and to Mary's chagrin England grew more Protestant under his brief rule. When Edward died unexpectedly in 1553, there was an arm wrestle for the throne. Edward, fearing that Mary would overturn his Protestant reforms, had tried to exclude his half-sisters from the line of succession in his last will and testament. In their place, Lady Jane Grey – daughter of the Duke of Northumberland – was put forward as rightful heir, but her claim was weak and short-lived. So, in the summer, Mary entered London as queen by popular consent.

But now she was in her late thirties and the question of issue became more important than ever. Without one, Elizabeth would succeed her and undo any progress she might make for Catholics in the realm. For a while, Reginald Pole (who would subsequently become Archbishop of Canterbury) and Edward Courtenay, Earl of Devon, were considered possible partners. But then Charles V suggested a marriage to his widowed son, Philip. Such was the fear of a Catholic Spanish prince marrying the English queen that there was an uprising – known as Wyatt's Rebellion after its leader, Thomas Wyatt – that saw Elizabeth implicated and imprisoned in the Tower of London.

The rebellion thwarted, Mary continued with her marriage plans. By law, Philip would be recognised as king of England for the duration of her reign but his powers were limited and England owed no military obligation to his homeland. In truth, here was another royal marriage in which the groom at least was utterly devoid of genuine passion and entered into it for purely strategic reasons. But Mary, too, hoped that the union would strengthen her political position at home and abroad.

They were wed in July 1554, just a couple of days after first meeting, with Mary assuming the additional titles of Queen of Naples and Jerusalem from her husband (he would also become King of Spain in 1556). The following year, Mary showed the indicators of being pregnant but it seems to have been a false pregnancy. Philip left England to head military expeditions overseas and Mary was reportedly bereft. Meanwhile, her reign was defined by religious conflict – the spiralling number of executions of prominent Protestants whom she believed had acted treacherously against her and the state earned her the nickname of 'Bloody Mary'.

When Philip returned in 1557, Mary again thought she had fallen pregnant but once more it was fruitless. Resigned to passing the throne on to Elizabeth, Mary died on 17 November 1558 at St James's Palace in London during an outbreak of influenza, though she may also have been suffering from ovarian cancer. 'I felt a reasonable regret for her death,' Philip commented to his sister, the height of the feelings he could muster for Mary.

The Letters

Mary's letters to Philip reveal two sides to her personality. The first missive was dispatched via an intermediary and served as an appeal to Philip's affections, imbued with a bride-to-be's hopes of a contented marriage. In truth, any feelings Mary harboured for a man she hardly knew were never reciprocated. The second letter retains a respectful and even affectionate tone in its last paragraph, but the bulk of it is a response to Philip's angry demands that she push for her sister Elizabeth to become the wife of the Prince of Savoy. Recognising that Elizabeth is now her likely heir, Mary rightly argues that Parliament would not allow the next in line to the throne to leave the realm in such circumstances. In refusing to act against the wishes of her parliament, Mary is drawing a line in the sand – her duties as monarch may not be superseded by her duties as a wife.

Letter 1:

Mary to Philip (20 April 1554, prior to their marriage in July)

Sir, my good and constant ally – Knowing that the ambassador of the emperor, my lord and good father, resident at my court was dispatching the bearer hereof to Your Highness; although you have not privately written to me since our alliance has been negotiated, so it is that, feeling myself so much obliged by the sincere and true affection that you bear me, which you have as much confirmed by deeds, as by the letters written to the said ambassador and by the negotiation that the Sieur d'Egmont and others, and the ambassadors of my said lord have managed, I could not omit signifying to you my good wishes and duty, which I have ever to communicate with you; and I thank you very humbly for so many good offices, and apprise you at the same time that the Parliament, which represents the estates of my kingdom, has heard the articles of our marriage without opposition, inasmuch as they find the conditions thereof honourable, advantageous and more than reasonable, which puts me in entire confidence, that your coming hither will be certain and agreeable.

And, hoping shortly to supply the remainder verbally, I will make an end at present, praying the Creator to grant you, my good and constant ally, to make your journey hither in prosperity and health, commending myself very affectionately and humbly to Your Highness. Your entirely assured and most obliged ally,

Mary

At London, 20th April

Letter 2:

Mary to Philip (c. 1557)

Monseigneur,

I have received the letters from Your Highness, by Francisco [an emissary], the 18th instant. Humbly thanking you for the same, especially as you are pleased to write you took mine in good part, which were, indeed I assure Your Highness, written with good intention; and, assuredly, seeing that yours was written with the same, I can say nothing more than to entreat Your Highness (seeing that you think it right that I examine my conscience to discover whether it is founded in truth or not) to name what persons Your Highness may think most proper to communicate with me on this affair, and I will willingly listen to them sincerely, whomsoever they may be.

Nevertheless, in my last letter to Your Highness, I made an offer to agree to the marriage provided I have the consent of this Realm, and so I will; but without such consent, I fear that neither Your Highness nor the Realm will be well served on this occasion.

For Your Highness will remember, that once I procured of myself, an opportunity of listening to Your Highness' friars, but they, and Alphonso [the king's confessor] propounded questions so obscure that, to my simple understanding, there was no comprehending them: as, for instance, 'Who was king in Adam's days?' and said, withal, 'That I was bound to conclude this marriage by an article in my creed' ...

Meantime, Your Highness has written in the said letters, that, if a Parliament shall go contrary, Your Highness will impute the fault to me.

I beg, in all humility, that Your Highness will defer this matter till your return, and then it will be manifest whether I am culpable or not. Otherwise, I shall live in apprehension of Your Highness' displeasure, which would be worse to me than death; for I have already begun to taste it too much, to my regret.

Wherefore, Monseigneur, in as humble ways as it is possible for me (being your very loyal and very obedient wife, which to be I confess myself justly obliged, and in my opinion more than any other woman, having such a husband as Your Highness is, without speaking of the multitude of your kingdoms, for which that is not my principal motive), I entreat Your Highness that we both pray to God, and put our first confidence in Him, that we may meet and live together. And that same God, in whose hand is the direction of the hearts of kings, will, I hope, without fail enlighten us in such manner, that all at last shall tend to His glory and your satisfaction.

Elizabeth I and Her Suitors

Elizabeth was born on 7 September 1533 at Greenwich Palace to Henry VIII and Anne Boleyn. She was the second child of Henry's to survive into adulthood, but first became heir to the throne as an infant when her half-sister, Mary, was declared illegitimate following the annulment of the marriage of Henry VIII to her mother, Catherine of Aragon.

Unlike her half-sister, Elizabeth was raised a Protestant. After her mother's execution, when she was still only two years old, Elizabeth was declared illegitimate and removed from the line of succession – the Act of Succession of 1544 later restored her claim to the throne. When Henry VIII died, Edward VI succeeded him, while the fourteen-year-old Elizabeth went to live with her father's last wife, Katherine Parr, and her new husband, Thomas Seymour, brother of another of her step-mothers, Jane Seymour. If that were not all complicated enough, Elizabeth herself had rejected a proposal of marriage from Thomas shortly after Henry's death and there is ample evidence to suggest that he sexually molested her while she lived under his roof – with or without his wife's acquiescence. He renewed his efforts to marry Elizabeth after Katherine's death in childbirth in 1548. These horrific experiences doubtless cast a shadow over the subsequent relationships Elizabeth forged with suitors in the years to come.

After Edward's unexpected death in 1553, Mary Tudor acceded to the throne. The religious tensions between the half-sisters – one avowedly Catholic, the other Protestant – was merely a microcosm of the faith wars playing out across the nation. Indeed, Elizabeth would be arrested and imprisoned for her role in a Protestant uprising, although how actively she had backed the action remains up for debate. By 1558, however, both Mary and her husband, Philip II of Spain, had come to terms with Elizabeth succeeding to the monarchy. She became queen at the age of twenty-five on Mary's death in November that year.

There was inevitable concern among England's ruling class that Elizabeth should promptly find a suitable husband and secure the line of succession. Elizabeth, though, would remain resolutely unmarried for the whole of her life. Yet this was not for an absence of suitors. Early in her reign, there was the prospect that she might marry Philip, Mary's widower, but Elizabeth turned down his proposal. The pair, unlikely allies as they were, nevertheless remained on good terms for some years before a steep deterioration in their relationship. Eric

XIV of Sweden was another promising candidate for a while, but few in the know doubted where her affections really lay – with Robert Dudley, a son of the Duke of Northumberland, who had been her friend since childhood. There were major hurdles to their union, however. For one, Dudley was already married, and for another, his father had played a pivotal role in trying to put Lady Jane Grey on the throne. That failed enterprise saw the Dudley fortunes decline, and many within the country remained suspicious of the family.

In 1560, Dudley's wife Amy passed away after a fall down some stairs. Despite natural suspicions of foul play, it was almost certainly an accidental death and was ruled as such. Elizabeth now seriously considered marrying Dudley, but several of her advisors made their unhappiness at the match known to her. She even suggested that Dudley might instead marry her cousin Mary, Queen of Scots, who many English Catholics had in mind for the English throne. Elizabeth thought a match could smooth matters between her and Mary and that the three might live together in England. He, though, rejected the idea out of hand. By the mid-1560s, Dudley, who the queen had made Earl of Essex, accepted he would never marry Elizabeth. Nonetheless, he remained her favourite and when he remarried in 1578, his new wife, Lettice Knollys, became something of a hate figure to the monarch.

Among other candidates for Elizabeth's hand were Archduke Charles of Austria, Frederick II of Denmark and even Ivan the Terrible of Russia. But after Dudley, arguably the most serious contender was Francis, Duke of Anjou, the son of France's King Henry II and Catherine de' Medici, who was somewhat dangled on a string for several years as negotiations for a match with Elizabeth, twenty-two years his senior, played out. As she grew older, Elizabeth actively made a virtue of her unmarried status and promoted – whether justifiably or not, we do not know – an aura of purity. Here was the unsullied Virgin Queen, married only to her subjects. 'And, in the end,' she once told Parliament, 'this shall be for me sufficient, that a marble stone shall declare that a queen, having reigned such a time, lived and died a virgin.' Privately, Elizabeth also came to recognise that while marriage could bring strategic advantage, it might also bring about conflict and disharmony. As she is reported to have said: 'If I follow the inclination of my nature, it is this: beggar woman and single, far rather than queen and married.'

In the event, Elizabeth has come to be regarded among the very greatest of English monarchs, and it is difficult to argue that her reputation suffered for lack of a spouse, even if it meant she was to be the last of the Tudors. Her reign was long and, despite a series of Catholic plots, remarkably stable. Here was a ruler who crafted her own legend. 'I know I have the body but of a weak and feeble woman,' she famously declared, 'but I have the heart and stomach of a king, and of a king of England too.' History was on her side as well. Alongside the naval triumph against the Spanish Armada (sold to her subjects as one of the greatest military achievements in history), her reign coincided with an age of English expansionism spearheaded by swashbuckling adventurers such as Francis Drake. It was also a time of unprecedented cultural production, with William Shakespeare and Christopher Marlowe in their pomp. Such is the stuff of fabled 'Golden Ages'.

Elizabeth died at Richmond Palace on 24 March 1603, to be succeeded by a moderately distant cousin, James VI of Scotland – the son of Mary, Queen of Scots, whose execution Elizabeth had authorised in 1587. Elizabeth departed the world as she had lived much of her life: alone. But for a woman who encouraged the 'Virgin Queen' mythology, there remains plenty of romantic intrigue around her.

The Letters: Thomas Seymour

This first batch of letters is doubtless the most troubling to a modern audience. They reveal the middle-aged Thomas Seymour seeking the hand in marriage of the thirteen-year-old Elizabeth, her father dead less than a month. Elizabeth's response – poised, polite yet firm – is thus all the more remarkable, and speaks very much of the age in which it was produced. It is worth remembering, too, that within a fortnight of Elizabeth rejecting him, Seymour was engaged to Katherine Parr. The third letter in this set was probably written while Elizabeth was living with her stepmother and her new husband, and was likely already suffering abuse at Seymour's hands. Written in response to a note of apology of his, for some minor service not properly rendered, it again demonstrates Elizabeth's restraint (tempered, perhaps, with real fear) and cool distance. Then comes the final missive, a definitive rejection of his renewed advances after the death of Katherine Parr.

Letter 1:

Thomas to Elizabeth (26 February 1547)

Madame – I wish that I were able by some enchantment to convey to this note the virtue of creating as much inclination in your heart towards me as mine is full of love for you. I beg you to pardon me the liberty that I am taking in revealing to you my sentiments so soon, and beg you to impute the boldness of which I am guilty, to your beauty, to your many charms and the excellent qualities that you possess, and to a certain enchantment over which I am not master. Everyone seeks to be happy, and Nature herself even bears us in that direction. But no one has ever longed for it so much as I, since today I have become so daring as to venture to lay claim to the greatest happiness that could come to any man, and to become possessed of the greatest treasure on Earth. I have so much regard for you, my beautiful Princess, that I have not dared to declare to you the fire with which I am being consumed for you, and the impatience of which I am possessed to convince you of my passion cannot allow me the time to wait until an opportunity presents itself. I come, then, to open my heart to you, wherein the image of your great qualities is so deeply engraven by the beautiful hands of the most ardent and pure love in the world, that I venture to hope one day to possess the original. If it is my good fortune to be able to inspire in you sentiments favourable towards me, and you will consent to marriage, you could assure yourself of having brought about the happiness of a man who will worship you till the tomb. Pardon me, once again, for the liberty that I take, since that which comes from a depth of good intention is ever excusable; just two lines, which I await from you, will inform me if I am to be happy or otherwise. Till then I am altogether yours,

Thomas (Admiral)

Letter 2:

Elizabeth to Thomas (27 February 1547)

My Lord Admiral – The letter you have written to me is the most obliging, and at the same time the most eloquent, in the world. And as I do not feel myself competent to reply to so many courteous expressions, I shall content myself with unfolding to you, in few words, my real sentiments. I confess to you that your letter, all elegant as it is, has very much surprised me; for, besides that neither my age nor my inclination allows me to think of marriage, I never could have believed that anyone would have spoken to me of nuptials, at a time when I ought to think of nothing but sorrow for the death of my father. And to him I owe so much, that I must have two years at least to mourn for his loss. And how can I make up my mind to become a wife before I shall have enjoyed for some years my virgin state, and arrived at years of discretion?

Permit me, then, my Lord Admiral, to tell you frankly that as there is no one in the world who more esteems your merit than myself, or who sees you with more pleasure as a disinterested person, so would I preserve to myself the privilege of recognising you as such, without entering into that strict bond of matrimony that often causes one to forget the possession of true merit. Let Your Highness be well persuaded that, though I decline the happiness of becoming your wife, I shall never cease to interest myself in all that can crown your merit with glory, and shall ever feel the greatest pleasure in being your servant and good friend,

Elizabeth

Letter 3:

Elizabeth to Thomas (c. 1547 or 1548)

My Lord – You needed not to send an excuse to me, for I could not mistrust the not fulfilling your promise to proceed from want of goodwill, but only that opportunity served not. Wherefore I shall desire you to think that a greater matter than this could not make me impute any unkindness in you, for I am a friend not won with trifles, nor lost with the like. Thus I commit you and your affairs into God's hand, Who keep you from all evil. I pray you to make my humble commendations to the queen's Highness.

Your assured friend to my little power,

Elizabeth

Letter 4:
Elizabeth to Thomas (1548)

My Lord – I have regarded the honour that you have made me till now as a result of your natural politeness, and as a mark of the zeal that you have for the memory of the late king, my father. But I am compelled to perceive, however, by the frequent visits that you have made that you have other thoughts, and if I had not perceived this myself, so many people have spoken to me of your conduct, that I certainly could not remain in ignorance, until I was reproached that I only refused you because I had thoughts of someone else. I beg you, therefore, my lord, to set your mind at rest on the matter, and be persuaded by the declaration that I make to you, that up till now I have not had the smallest thought of marrying, and that if the time should come for me to think thereof, which I believe never will come, you would be the first person to whom I should make known my resolution.

The Letters: Edward Courtenay

The following trio of letters is of disputed authenticity. The missives purport to be correspondence between Elizabeth and a courtier, Edward Courtenay, the Earl of Devon – a man who was variously tipped to marry either Mary Tudor or Elizabeth. However, he was implicated in the failed Wyatt's Rebellion – an anti-Catholic response to Mary's marriage to Philip of Spain. He and Elizabeth were both accused of helping to incite the uprising and were duly imprisoned. Elizabeth blamed Courtenay in part for her incarceration and their hitherto close friendship quickly fell away. These letters, the first two of which were supposedly composed a year before the rebellion, were presented as authentic by certain historians writing in the century after Elizabeth's reign, but others have claimed them to be forgeries.

Letter 1:
Elizabeth to Edward (1553)
My Lord – I do not doubt that you love me, but I fear that this love may do you injury. This is the reason that compels me to hide the liking that I have for you and gives me little

hope; but I am aware that a generous heart like yours knows how to love even till suspicion, and that jealousy gives additional charms to love. I am sure that when you reflect on the risk to which you expose yourself of losing a crown, or at least a very high position in the realm because you do not care to respond to the wishes and the love that the queen bears to you, but you prefer to follow that which inspires in you an amorous passion for her who wishes that her power and her fortunes were as great as to be able to make you happy. I am convinced, as I have said, that when you really consider your own interests, you will separate yourself as far from me as I would wish to be near to you, and that I am thoroughly certain of this by the great esteem that I have of your virtues. Consider, my dear Lord, that love very often blinds reason and that it overthrows into a whirlpool of misery all who follow, and then steals away and leaves them to help themselves out as best they may. Meditate a little on these warnings, which come from a heart that only seeks your welfare, since it is certain that I would rather deprive myself of all than do you any harm. Do me the justice to be persuaded that I love you more than you do me, and that I await you impatiently so as to declare to you what prudence does not suffer me to write.

    Elizabeth

Letter 2:

Edward to Elizabeth (1553)

Madame — I would that I had two hearts, so as to sacrifice one to your good counsels. But having only one destiny to make me happy by the love that I have for you, it would kill me to make it live for aught else. I beseech you, my beloved Princess, to be persuaded that neither fortune nor crown can shake the love that I have for you only, and neither the power nor the violence of the world is capable of tearing from my heart the resolution that I have made to devote myself to your service. I know that it is very rash of me to dare, without any merits of my own, to inspire to the greatest happiness on Earth, which is to love the most beautiful and the most accomplished princess in the universe. I am rejoiced, however, madame, to learn that you are aware that love is blind, because that makes me hope that you will not find so strange the rashness of a heart that only would know how to love an object that is worthy of crowns and realms. I gratify my pride in reflecting incessantly on your worth and I keep up my hope by convincing myself more and more that I am incapable of loving anyone else but you, having resolved not to desire any happiness in the world other than that which will come from you. Forgive, if you please, the very great liberty that he takes who cannot live without loving you nor die except as your faithful servant,

Courtenay

This last letter in the trilogy was written a few days prior to Courtenay's death in Padua from an unspecified ailment. He had gone into exile in the Venetian Republic the previous year.

Letter 3:

Edward to Elizabeth (September 1556)

My Dear Princess – Finding myself with a sharp attack of fever that is so violent as to threaten me with death, notwithstanding that I have only felt ill since yesterday, I have determined to take advantage of a short interval of freedom from the delirium the fever causes me, so as to have the honour of writing to you, not knowing from one moment to another how my illness may turn out. I beseech you to consider how great must be the love that I have for you, since I do not allow myself to cease from remembering you and writing to you in these last moments of my life, which ought to be devoted entirely to the good of my soul. I beg of you to be persuaded, my dear Princess, that the entire love that I have for you has been pure and sincere, and that I have not had any other thought than to be able to have one day the happiness of becoming your husband, by just and legitimate means; but Providence who has not deemed me deserving of such great happiness, has punished me for my rashness, for which I ask your pardon, my dear Princess, as well as for everything else in respect of which I might have unknowingly offended you, since I have never been capable of doing so

consciously. From the first day when you did me the honour
of showing me some favour, I determined to be faithful
to you till death; and it is indeed proper in the condition
in which I find myself, that in order to fulfil that pledge, I
should devote to you the last hours of my life. I am dying in
exile, without having committed any worse crime than that of
having supported the interests of her who bestowed upon me
the honour of loving me, and of allowing me to love her: and
in the depth of the illness wherein I am placed I can find no
other relief than the pleasure of writing to you this letter. I
hope that you will have the graciousness to accept it with that
same royal generosity with which you have condescended
to love me, and that you will accept also the two enclosed
rings that I send you, and that I may place them again in the
same hands that gave them to me. I could not resolve to be
deprived of them, if I believed that I had much longer to live;
it is for that reason that I have given orders that this letter
is to be sent to you only after my death. The fever that takes
hold upon me does not allow me to say any more to you, and
compels me to end with the desire that I had been able to
obtain for a little longer the pleasure of writing to you. My
illness is too violent to last long, and very soon, I expect that
it will end in death. Goodbye, my dear Princess.

The Letters: Francis, Duke of Anjou

Now, a collection of letters to Francis, Duke of Anjou, written while Elizabeth was in her forties and he in his twenties. Elizabeth affectionately referred to him as her 'frog'. He courted her in person and there was certainly genuine chemistry between them. But the idea that Elizabeth might marry a French Catholic did not play well at home and the letters attest to the long and protracted dealings carried out by intermediaries. Ultimately, Elizabeth somewhat reluctantly concluded that it was politic to end marriage plans. Nonetheless, she was inconsolable when news reached her of his death from illness after he had waged a disastrous military campaign in the Netherlands in 1583.

Letter 1:

Elizabeth to Francis (16 January 1579)

Monsieur – After the long-delayed journey of Monsieur Symey he has now, thanks to God, arrived in life and good health ... This gentleman has delivered to me your letters worthy not of parchment but of being written in marble, for which, as for more things besides, you make me too indebted ... I would counsel you to take advice from the wisest and in those in whom you place the greatest confidence if you do not think that your honour would be dimmed by taking the journey into this country without the assurance of your desire. And if in the slightest you think it would, I would not dim it for all the gold in the world ... I cannot imagine that they will think it convenient, yet for all that, I will not show myself so presumptuous as to prejudice their wise advice ... I have bored you too much with so wearisome a letter, begging you to pardon the length of the same, beseeching the Creator, after my very cordial commendations to you, monsieur, that you may live the years of Nestor to the confusion of the machinations of your enemies, so as to be able always to vanquish them.

Your very assured good sister and cousin,
Elizabeth R.

Letter 2:

Elizabeth to Francis (8 February 1579)

Could you imagine, monsieur, that any other regret could equal that which you have caused me by your last letters, from which I learn that the fault into which you have never yet during your life fallen, must be imputed? I do indeed see that your thoughts were far away from mine. I shall never need to be rebuked about that which concerns the honour of a prince, since I hold their compact as sacred, and have had no thought of violating the same in a matter of the smallest consequence: so that if we covenant otherwise, I shall consider myself unworthy of the rank that I hold. But, monsieur, it seems to me that the error of not having

understood what was in my mind has entirely escaped you ...
I see very clearly the rare constancy reposing in your heart,
which is not diminished by some shadow of ingratitude that
is proof enough to assure me of your sincere affection. Listen,
now, if you please: my intention was that when the articles
had been concluded and given under the condition that if
I deemed it convenient for both of us to pass over them,
finding all the details quite in order, then the commissioners
might come in accordance with my advertisement to you
and the king. And seeing that there was great difficulty in
rendering it agreeable to my subjects in regard to certain
matters already detailed in my last letters, I employed some
boldness with regard to you to indicate the disposition of
our people than altogether to put an end to the matter,
thinking that you would rather determine either not to risk
your repose, which could not make me easy, or being content
for the love of me, you would conquer me by love ... I am
not unaware my dearest that certain people, among whom
I suspect Simié [Jean Simié, Anjou's servant who carried
out much of the wooing of Elizabeth on his master's behalf.
She referred to him as the 'monkey'], will say that there are
only two or three that persuade me of these impediments;
believe me that if everything is taken into consideration
which Simié can say to you, there is not one of those whom
you can suspect that has so much merit as to hold a place in
my good grace so that I owe him my love. I know all the time

that they are men who can easily deceive. This is enough to one so wise as yourself. If these words are not clear to you, let me know, through the medium of our monkey. I promise you, that if I had thought that such a paraphrase could be made of the text of my letter, I would rather be killed ... For you know, monsieur, that had you wished to keep back the commissioners, and, in consideration of the difficulties, wished to go no further in the matter, then the articles would have had no value. And on your replying, the articles could be ended ... However, as for myself, I am assured that I must be advised first before going any further, without knowing your final answer; and whilst awaiting this, I shall finish this letter, with the desire to be commended to your usual good opinion of me, imploring the Creator to preserve you always in good life and a long one.

Written at Westminster, 8th of February

Letter 3:

Elizabeth to Francis (1579)

Monsieur – The necessity of the cause has compelled me, contrary to my custom, to send a letter to the king first, before informing you thereof. You will pardon this deceit, which I have not committed with the intention of hindering too much the commissioners ... If he should show himself reluctant to effect your cause, you will have an opportunity of estimating the desire that he possesses for your greatness.

I am sending you my letter as to one with whom I share my follies, hoping as much in the goodness of your nature as I believe that your chiefest business will be dealt with as conveniently as possible for your own contentment ... As to you, monsieur, every one can justly be assured that you dispose of all other thoughts solely to make me yours: by your unerring constancy you will have well deserved what I hold engraven in my heart, to be your slave for ever.

Letter 4:

Elizabeth to Francis (17 January 1580)

My delaying so much, my dearest, to acknowledge the countless ways that increase my indebtedness to you, can rightly render me unworthy of such honourable treatment. But the very great pain that I have had in my throat for this past fortnight without ceasing will have the power, I hope, of blotting out such a conception. And now, finding myself a little better, behold me offering my humble thanks for having shown us a clear rock, against which neither the tempests of false persuasions, nor the storm of wicked tongues have had the ability to move the constancy of your affection, of which I confess that I am indeed unworthy for any perfection that I retain. And as for this, it seems to me as much more excellent as the opportunity is the more rare. Of one thing I rejoice, that you are so well provided with good advice, that you will not be ignorant of some of my replies in defence, so as to assure me of not being found worse than they have found me already. And in regard to that, being so well warned, you will have thoroughly made up your mind, or will not run the risk. And pray God grant you the grace of a clear insight so as to penetrate the depth of their conspiracies and that I do not live to be a means of your discontentment. It is so difficult at this time to recognise the difference between what seems and what actually is, that I long for the wisdom of Solomon to dwell in your mind to separate the false from the sincere ... But now I am dreaming on just as fiddles make one to dream, not having slept well. I have received news from the king that the commissioners are getting ready ... In short I beg you to forgive this tedious letter and accept my very humble thanks for the offer that you make me of disposing of the cause of Simié, as it will seem best to me, assuring you that I have never any care to give you advice that will betray your honour: rather would I die. I am not so biased that I forget you ... With my very affectionate commendations.

P.S. – I beg you to let me know your good pleasure by this messenger, who will return in haste.

Letter 5:

Elizabeth to Francis (1580)

My Dearest – The too long delay that I have made of this messenger makes me so ashamed that I can scarcely dare to ask pardon. But when you learn of the very great pain

in the head that I have had for ten days, this will be I hope
sufficient excuse to purge my guilt, begging you to believe
that nonetheless I have not been negligent of your affairs,
as the gentleman will tell you at greater length. On reading
through the articles again, which it has pleased you to send
me, directed through the Low Countries, there is not one
that pleases me more than a denunciation made by the king
against the King of Spain, as being the most assured root
and basis of your action in this country. See, if you please,
that to undertake so important a project it is essential
not only that this be commenced, but regarded in such a
manner as one will protect it. And as to this, wealth is the
true sinew of war, and if that is but limited it is necessary
that the enterprise must be the same. And remember the
length of this civil war, and the opportunities in going forth
of draining from the depth their means; also having regard
to your own territory, albeit that it is greater than ever a
son of France possessed, nevertheless I doubt if it will be
adequate for so great an expense; thus I desire, since I am
not sufficiently wise to advise you in so important a matter,
that you beseech the king to assure you of the assistance
in abandoning the friendship of the King of Spain, having
a greater regard to France than to Castille. And methinks
that the king must have a great regard so to do if he does not
listen too attentively to the hangers-on of the Spanish ducats,
or to those who, preserving their greatness, take no thought

in the matter. I suspect that the king does not see that this
provision that he has made will not be an obstacle. His
victory in Portugal has caused him too much misfortune that
I fear he will feel it very much, when he finds himself unable:
but if not, avoid such counsel, when any reparation would
be wished for too late. I understand that you have asked the
king so as to learn his answer, which I hope that by now you
have received, and when I shall receive it, I shall be able to
send you my reply more privately. And I shall not fail to let
you know with all possible haste, not wishing that your affairs
should be delayed by mine, assuring you that I shall have as
much consideration for them as for mine own.

Letter 6:

Elizabeth to Francis (17 March 1581)

To Monsieur D'Anjou, my dearest cousin,

The honour that you pay me is very great, in frequently
letting me hear from you by your letters, but the ease that
I thereby obtain exceeds that honour very much, since I do
not desire anything so much as the continuation of your good
opinion towards me, thanking you very humbly for the sweet
flowers gathered by your hand ... and I vow to you that never
has a gift travelled better, for the greenness has remained as
fresh as if it were gathered this very moment, and indicates to
me most vividly your lively affection towards me, and I hope
never to give you just cause for it to fade. Monsieur, I have

been anxious to lose neither a leaf nor a flower for all the other jewels that I possess. I beg you to believe that I cannot express the joy that this bearer brings me, and forgive me if he has not returned sooner, whilst awaiting my messenger, by whom I have received a letter from you, in which you make me immensely indebted, nevertheless, by so many honourable offerings, all full of affection: which, although I cannot wholly repay, yet I shall not fail to acknowledge by every means in my power. I am glad, monsieur, that you assure yourself of me, as of the most faithful friendship that a prince ever had ... There has not been a word written with the intention of separating me from your good affection but what I was not in the least ignorant of. But what I must think I do not know, except you make me ever your debtor, and I shall never think otherwise of you than the same honour and innumerable virtues. As the Creator knows, Whom, with my most cordial commendations, I beg to grant you all the honour and happiness in the world, beseeching you to hold me ever in your good graces.

At Westminster, this 17th of March, your ever indebted, Elizabeth R.

This next letter was written after a force led by the duke had wrested Cambrai from Habsburg control.

Letter 7:

Elizabeth to Francis (1581)

My Dearest – I see clearly that God answers the prayers
of old women, by His having assisted you with His hand,
and winning in such a manner your glory and honour, as I
myself have on my bended knees prayed for it, that is to say
that you might be allowed to achieve so fine a feat without
injury to your person, without much bloodshed, and
without any credit to the enemy, and with their shameful
retreat. I do not doubt otherwise, my dearest, that you do
not now so much the more marvel at the Divine goodness,
which has surprised the human understanding by seeing
so mighty a force gathered together without the king's
command and without his especial protection, so mighty
a multitude ruled without an expert deputy, and, what is
more, governed by yourself alone, without the assistance of
any old experienced captains, having no counsellors, as far
as I can learn, by whom you could be served in the time of
your greatest need. Oh what failings and defects are these
for affording some hope that your affairs may proceed in
good order and nevertheless since, as if by a miracle, God
has given you this extraordinary favour, never tempt Him
(I most humbly beseech you) once more, without being
better equipped; for, if the sequel had turned out unhappy,
there is no one in the world, who loves you better, who
had not condemned you as worthy by such a beginning

to receive punishment. They say that the war that is well planned is half won. At this juncture, monseigneur, now that you have carried out most worthily your promise to the people of Cambrai, who have received it by good merit, be content with this, without taking any more risks, considering that the time of winter is that in which soldiers may rest, and princes may withdraw from war. It is the time for them, closetted in their chambers, to put their affairs in order and by that means to preserve what has been won, allowing these troops that come to overthrow you to be the means of injuring others by their coming and allow them to be beaten by this same means ... You see how the affection for your welfare transports me, begging you to let me know your pardon, and to believe that although I have not the intellect to serve you with advice, yet I have the soul that wishes you the best of everything that could be desired, as God knows, Whom I implore to give you a hundred years of life.

I cannot return the smallest part of the very humble thanks that I owe to you for having so much honoured the Garter, which is of so little value, that it could not ever be worthy of such a bearer, and I assure you that the leg that wears it will ever go most willingly before whatever danger may threaten you.

Letter 8:

Elizabeth to Francis (1581)

My Dearest – To begin to relate the many obligations that, from one day to another, your kind acts towards me afford, would cause me to enter into a labyrinth far too intricate; the number, however, is so infinite that I could not say more, did it not pain me too much to see my inability to answer in a measure so incapable of being measured. And I thank you very humbly, lastly, for your trust in me, which makes me astounded at a constancy so rare, that is not moved by the temper of a number of malcontents who are not slow to thwart your wishes. And in the first place to reply to the honour that it has pleased Your Grace to offer me by your presence, although I cannot hold anyone more dear, nor be so satisfied with aught else in the world ... being anxious that you should not be exposed to the danger of some accident that could befall you by the way, thinking myself too happy that such a thought abides in your heart, which increases my welfare and more tightly grasps me moreover till the arrival of the commissioners ... It is to you, monsieur, that I declare before God in good faith whilst thinking, in the time to come, of the irksomeness that a woman so different from you in years may cause you, not wishing to live to weave for you so hard a penance, but if no admonition can turn you aside from risking such a misfortune, I cannot tell you that I was not anxious that

this should be which would give you the most honour ...
Ending this all too lengthy a letter, commending myself
above all to your good graces, beseeching the Lord God to
grant you a hundred years of life.

In response to the failure of these marriage negotiations,
Elizabeth is believed to have written the following plaintive
poem, entitled 'On Monsieur's Departure'.

I grieve and dare not show my discontent;
I love, and yet am forced to seem to hate;
I do, yet dare not say I ever meant;
I seem stark mute, but inwardly do prate.
I am, and not; I freeze and yet am burned,
Since from myself another self I turned.

My care is like my shadow in the sun –
Follows me flying, flies when I pursue it,
Stands, and lies by me, doth what I have done;
His too familiar care doth make me rue it.
No means I find to rid him from my breast,
Till by the end of things it be suppressed.

Some gentler passion slide into my mind,
For I am soft and made of melting snow;
Or be more cruel, Love, and so be kind.

Let me or float or sink, be high or low;
Or let me live with some more sweet content,
Or die, and so forget what love e'er meant.

These final letters concern surely the greatest love of Elizabeth's life, Robert Dudley, Earl of Leicester. These come from their later years, after the initial passion of their youth had long passed. Nonetheless, they speak of the deep affection each retained for the other after lifetimes of uncommon respective drama. The first note is from Elizabeth, written to Dudley after he had gone to the Netherlands (in support of the Dutch Revolt against Habsburg rule) and accepted the title of Governor-General in direct contravention of her orders. She was initially utterly furious but this letter illustrates how he, above all others, was able to command her affection even in light of the severest provocations. The final letter, meanwhile, was written just a few days before Dudley's death, back in England, on 4 September 1588. Elizabeth kept it until her own death in a chest beneath her bed, inscribed 'his Last lettar'.

Letter 1:

Elizabeth to Robert (19 July 1586)

Rob – I am afraid you will suppose by my wandering writings, that a midsomer moon hath taken large possession of my brains this month, but you must needs take things as they come in my head though order be left behind me. When I remember your request to have a discrete and honest man, that may carry my mind and see how all goes there, I have chosen this bearer whom you know, and have made good trial of ... I am sure you can credit him and so I will be short with these few notes. First that Counte Morice and Counte Hollocke [leaders of the Dutch anti-Spanish resistance] find themselves trusted of you, esteemed of me and to be careful regarded if ever peace should happen, and of that assure them on my word, that yet never deceived any ... Now will I end that do imagine I talk still with you, and therefore loathly say farewell ōō [Elizabeth's name of affection for Dudley was 'Eyes' and she used 'ōō' to symbolise it] though ever I pray God bless you from all harm and save you from all foes with my million and legion of thanks for all your pains and cares. As you know, ever the same.

E. R.

Letter 2:

Robert to Elizabeth (29 August 1588)

I most humbly beseech your majesty to pardon your poor old servant to be this bold in sending to know how my gracious lady doth and what ease of her late pain she finds, being the chiefest thing in the world I do pray for and for her to have good health and long life. For my own poor case, I continue still your medicine and find it amended much better than with any other thing that hath been given me. Thus hoping to find perfect cure at the bath, with the continuance of my wanted prayer for *Dudley* Majesty's most happy preservation. I humbly kiss your foot. From your old lodging at Rycott this Thursday morning ready to take on my journey.

By your most faithful and obedient servant,

R. Leycester

P.S. Even as I had written thus much I received Your Majesty's token by young Tracey.

Mary, Queen of Scots and Lord Bothwell

Mary Stuart was born at Linlithgow Palace in Scotland on 8 December 1542, the daughter of James V of Scotland and Mary of Guise. She inherited the Scottish throne after her father died when she was just six days old. As a great-niece of Henry VIII via her paternal grandmother, Margaret Tudor, she had a claim to the English throne that posed a threat to the claims of both Mary Tudor and Elizabeth I, who had variously been delegitimised by Henry and removed from the line of succession by Edward VI.

Regents ruled Scotland while Mary grew up, with the Catholic Cardinal Beaton and the Protestant Earl of Arran engaged in a ferocious power struggle. In a bid to unite the English and Scottish crowns and lessen Scotland's close ties to Catholic France, Henry VIII suggested a marriage between Mary (who was at the time six months old) and his son, Edward, which was to take place when Mary turned ten. However, the Scottish parliament rejected the plan, prompting Henry to launch a series of raids north of the border.

Scotland turned to France for protection and a treaty was agreed with the French king, Henry II, that Mary should marry his then infant son, the dauphin Francis. Mary was subsequently relocated to the French Court to be raised until both she and Francis were of an age to be married. The couple eventually wed in April 1558.

When Elizabeth I came to the English throne in 1558, many Catholics rallied around Mary as the true heir. Her father-in-law, Henry II, even proclaimed Francis and Mary as king and queen of England. Henry died the following year from injuries sustained whilst jousting and so the still teenage Francis became king of France. For the time being, life seemed good for Mary. She was young, accomplished and much admired for her beauty. She also seems to have been genuinely in love with her husband. But tragedy was to stalk her. In 1560, Francis died from complications resulting from an ear infection. His brother, Charles, took the French throne and Mary found herself subject to the whim of the regent, her mother-in-law Catherine de' Medici – one of the few people seemingly immune to Mary's charms.

Mary returned to her native Scotland in the summer of 1561. It was not much of a homecoming, though, as France was by then her real home. Moreover, she walked into a political minefield. The nation was tearing itself apart as to whether Protestantism or Catholicism should prevail, so Mary's Catholicism naturally and automatically aroused the suspicions of a significant part of the population. On the other hand, her relative tolerance for Protestantism in the realm incurred the anger of many Catholics. Then there was Elizabeth in England, who kept a wary eye on this potential rival for her throne.

Marriage inevitably became a means of shoring up Mary's regime. An early attempt to unite her with Archduke Charles of Austria failed, as she had not given consent for negotiations, while Philip II of Spain put an end to suggestions that she marry his heir apparent, Don Carlos. Elizabeth, meanwhile, hoped that she might keep tabs on Mary by marrying her off to her favourite, Robert Dudley, until Dudley refused the move. One apparently besotted court poet, Pierre de Boscosel de Chastelard, was even discovered underneath Mary's bed in 1563, from where he was said to be planning to spring out in order to declare his feelings.

However, it would be a half-cousin, Henry Stuart, Lord Darnley – a man well connected in English and Scottish aristocracy – whom she would marry next. The wedding was held in July 1565 but it quickly proved a very unhappy union. Elizabeth I was angered that she had not been asked for permission (given Darnley's position within English society) while leading Scottish Protestants – including Mary's half-brother, the Earl of Moray – resented the Catholic alliance. On top of that, Mary's initial infatuation soon waned as Darnley's true character emerged. He was jealous and power-hungry, taking it badly when Mary refused him the right to retain the throne in the event of her predeceasing him. He also became convinced that she was having an affair with her secretary David Rizzio. Darnley entered into a pact with a group of her Protestant enemies, with the result that, in March 1566, Rizzio was brutally murdered in front of the pregnant Mary (there were rumours that Rizzio might be the father) at Holyrood Palace in Edinburgh.

Mary gave birth to a son, James, in June but by then her marriage was doomed. Mary certainly discussed the possibility of divorce with her advisors, but matters were taken out of her hands. In February 1567, Darnley was recuperating from illness in a house in a former abbey, Kirk o' Field. Early one morning, there was a huge explosion at the property and Darnley was discovered dead in the garden, having apparently been strangled. Mary, Moray and others all came under suspicion, but it was Lord Bothwell who was put on trial for the crime. Acquitted in April, by May he was married to Mary.

The true nature of Mary and Bothwell's relationship has been a subject of eternal fascination to historians. We know that Mary was travelling from a visit to her son in Sterling back to Edinburgh in late April 1567 when she was effectively abducted by Bothwell and a large party of his men. She was then taken to Dunbar before the pair returned to Edinburgh for their marriage rites. It is sometimes alleged that Bothwell raped Mary in Dunbar as a means of securing his claim upon her and the throne. Others, though, have suggested that theirs was a long-standing love affair and that the 'abduction' was undertaken with Mary's cooperation. Alas for Mary, the marriage itself was again not to be a happy one. Catholics disapproved of her marriage to a Protestant, while pretty much everyone questioned her union to a man accused of murdering her previous spouse. Under such strain, it is hardly surprising that – regardless of the origins of the marriage – Mary and Bothwell were soon locked into a cycle of upset and arguments.

By July, twenty-six discontented peers had formed an army and arrested Mary, imprisoning her in Loch Leven Castle. There, later in the month, she miscarried twins and within days was forced to abdicate the throne in favour of her infant son, James. The Earl of Moray ruled as regent and Bothwell was sent into exile. Mary, meanwhile, escaped her captivity in 1568 and fled to England. However, Elizabeth I was wary of assisting her in the battle to regain her crown, and instead an inquiry was established to look into the question of Mary's involvement in Darnley's death. Mary refused to acknowledge the authority of the inquiry, which failed to find definitively for or against her. In the meantime, the Duke of Norfolk sought to become her next husband, resulting in Elizabeth imprisoning him.

Mary was constantly associated with plots against Elizabeth, even as she spent long years incarcerated. There was, for example, the Ridolfi Plot to unseat Elizabeth in 1571, then a plan by Pope Gregory XIII to have Mary married off to the Dutch governor-general in order to launch an invasion of England from the Netherlands, and then the Babington Plot of 1586 aimed at assassinating Elizabeth and replacing her with Mary. She was implicated in this last scheme by an intercepted letter, which led to her facing trial for treason. Convicted on 25 October 1586, Elizabeth dithered about signing her execution order – fearful of its political reper- cussions – but Mary was beheaded at Fotheringay Castle in Northamptonshire on 8 February 1587.

The Letters

Here is a collection of some of the most dramatic, incen- diary and disputed regal love correspondence in existence. The letters were produced by the Earl of Moray as evidence against Mary at the inquiry into Darnley's death held in 1568. Moray by then was regent of Scotland on behalf of James VI and thus had good reason to keep Mary far from the throne. The missives have become known as the Casket Letters, as they are said to have been found in a silver casket bearing the monogram of Francis II. Various witnesses attested at the time that they were written in Mary's hand. Mary herself claimed they were forgeries. Others have wondered if they were written by her but doctored by another hand. The story they tell is of a long-running love affair with Bothwell, almost perpetual intrigues and, most devastatingly for Mary, her foreknowledge of the plot to kill her husband, Lord Darnley.

Letter 1:

Mary to Lord Bothwell (c. mid-1563)

You complain of me my dear Bothwell without cause; did you know what insurmountable difficulties attend a person of my station in the pursuit of an affair such as ours, you would not blame but pity me, all my moments are taken up with consultations. The distractions of the times overwhelm me – I ought to exchange this soft and gentle nature of mine for one all rough and masculine, to be able to cope with the oppositions I daily meet with – besides the Lord Darnley is perpetually with me, pretends to testify his passion by his jealousy, and back'd by that assuming arbitress of my fate the English queen, already takes upon him the authority of a husband. What can I do, torn and divided between different factions, both equally pernicious to their sovereign's interest? Yet in spite of the contending storms, in spite of business cares, and all my vast fatigues, still does my heart find room for love. Yes, I protest my ever dear Bothwell, that for a humble life with you, I gladly would exchange this load of greatness and throw it to those who seem ambitious of it, this gaudy burden of a crown. But even that is a privilege denied me; I must either continue to reign or cease to live. My power is all that can protect my Bothwell; should I relinquish that, or want the means of preserving you, it is not the pretended friendship of the ever-changing Murray [alternative spelling of Moray, Mary's half-brother] would afford you any shelter: do not therefore impute it to the want of impatience to see you, that I still delay your coming to Edinburgh; 'tis for the future repose of us both that I command you to tarry yet longer where you are. But methinks I need not any arguments to convince you that it is wholly your interest I study. Too precious have been the proofs I have given you of my tenderness for you to doubt the sincerity of it, nor do I believe you want sense or gratitude to acknowledge what I have done for you. Time, however, must be the touchstone of the hearts of both – write to me as usual; believe me, all the consolation your unhappy queen enjoys is in the hearing from you; till fate allows us the blessing of a nearer conversation, which I hope and pray may be sooner than you expect, and as swift as my desires – a legion of angels attend and be your guard from all exterior harms and keep you ever faithful to

M. R.

P.S. I forgot to warn you of my Lord Herris; he designs you a visit, it can be for no other reason than to pry into your behaviour – be cautious of yourself before him, farewell.

Letter 2:

Mary to Lord Bothwell (c. mid-1563)

It is in a transport proportionable to my late uneasiness
that I now command the presence of my dear Bothwell
– the greatest part of my anxieties are over. Elizabeth has
changed her mind in favour of Lord Darnley, and I shall
be persecuted no more with her menaces or persuasions
on his score; Murray also declares himself an enemy to
the match, and I shall have the double satisfaction of
obliging my subjects and myself. But oh, there remains a
greater felicity in store for me; I shall not only be eased of
the solicitations of the man I hate, but enjoy with more
security than ever the society of him I love. The council
seems perfectly satisfied of your innocence as to the late
troubles; you will have a public mandate to recall you;
but I cannot restrain my impatience from sending you
this harbinger of our approaching happiness. Be secret,
however, I conjure you; a too quick discovery of your
contentment might yet ruin all – always remember this,
that the favourites of princes have as many observers as
eyes upon them – I learned this maxim from Catherine
de' Medici, to wear a countenance the reverse of my heart
– proposals frequently are made for no other reasons, than
to sound the inclinations of the persons to whom they
are offered; that politick queen therefore never discloses
either the pleasure or discontent she conceives at what she

hears, but leaving it to spring out of the reality, fathoms
the whole of the design without giving, even those who
think themselves at the very bottom of her secrets, liberty
to know the least of her thoughts: it is also by this means
that Elizabeth circumvents all the plots of her enemies;
and this in fine is the only security of a great and envied
person. Dissemble therefore, my dear Bothwell, with all
the world but me, who, I do believe, will be most pleased
when most I know your heart. See the confidence that
love inspires, jealousy and suspicion are passions I am
utterly a stranger to, but in the affairs of state, I confess I
have vanity enough to assure myself the man I condescend
to favour in the manner I have done you, cannot but be
mine. As for the divorce, you write to me concerning,
I would not have you think of it as yet; the times are at
present too much unsettled, and your wife has powerful
friends. Strengthen first your own interest, which may be
a means to weaken hers, and leave to me and your good
friend the Bishop of Ross to manage that thereafter; we
have already laid the scheme, and I am certain that worthy
man will not fail to perform the part enjoined him, to
the satisfaction of both. In the meantime I would not
have you give the least hint of your design: but of this we
shall have leisure to talk at your arrival. I have these three
days waited an opportunity to convey to you the tender
meanings of my soul, and must not waste the precious

moment in dull narrations. No time is pleasing to me
that is not spent in giving you new demonstrations of my
affections; well may I err in the rules of government and
state, when all my thoughts are taken up with love; and yet
perhaps I should be less capable than I am, if my concern
for the establishment of your happiness did not make me
now and then apply myself to those maxims that alone can
have the power to fix it. The ambition I have to make you
great, keeps alive my desire of continuing so myself.

The sceptre I am very certain would soon grow too
unwieldy for the weakness of my hand, were it not for
the charming hope I should shortly have the means of
transferring it into yours, 'tis there I wish to see it shine, and
look on myself but as the steward of a glorious relic. I do
believe, however, that there are joys in my power to bestow
infinitely more powerful to you than this, but I think not
my heart and person sufficient rewards for the merits of
my Bothwell, and long for the happy hour when I may give
a kingdom in dowry with my love: till then I cannot say my
joy is complete, nor will I ever rest till this, the supremest
desire my soul can know, is accomplished. I am now going to
council where I have ordered it so that the Earl of Hamilton,
who I know your enemy, shall be accused of things which,
for a time at least, shall deprive him of that power of giving
any interruption to happiness I propose to myself in the
enjoyment of my dear Bothwell's conversation: adieu –

expect in a few days to be called to court and to the impatient arms of

   M. R.

This next letter was written shortly after Elizabeth had suggested Mary marry Elizabeth's great love, Robert Dudley.

Letter 3:

Mary to Lord Bothwell (c. early 1564)

What a sudden turn in our affairs! Good God! How are the face of all things altered! Scarce have I courage to report the story – but you, alas, are but too well acquainted with the misfortune in general, though the particulars cannot yet have reached you: I am forever doomed to be the vassal of the English queen, the tool of her cursed policy, the property of her ambition, without a friend to aid me. She writes me now that the reasons for breaking off the match with Darnley were because she thinks Leicester more worthy of my bed and crown! Leicester raised but by her partial favour, and long the mirror of her loosest wishes, must now be recompensed with the Scottish Crown, but it shall perish first, though Murray and the faction again threaten to take up arms; though the remainder of the Gordon race rejoice in this opportunity of revenge, and all I have endured nor all I can endure, shall frighten me to an act so loathed, so scorned, no, if not decreed for Bothwell, I will be for no other: in this world I will be mistress of myself, as for the rest let fate dispose. I am grown weary of the light, and almost would resign that life they make so wretched by perpetual troubles.

Attempt not to appear in Edinburgh, I entreat you, where all things being in confusion, in this universal hurry, you may fall a victim to the malice of your enemies. I am now more than ever fearful of your betraying those secret practices he formerly entrusted to your care, and that he privately conspires against your life!

Hamilton gave me some hints of it the other day, and Douglas afterwards in heat of blood occasioned by a debate between them in my presence confirmed it: all are false! All are traitors to their queen! Oh, Bothwell, where is one faithful friend to be chosen out among a thousand base designers? I aim not at increase of power, oppress not my poor subjects by exorbitant taxations, nor envy the provinces my neighbours rule; all I desire is to possess in peace the little territories I was born to govern, and that is denied me. Sure I was born to everlasting cares! Like hydra heads, one no sooner disappears, than another rises in its room, and drives me from repose. I am in too much distraction to say much at present; but the person who brings you this has a commission to inform you of all the circumstances of this unexpected blow. I can only tell you that I am, as ever, wholly devoted to the interests of my dear Bothwell, and will yet some way or other complete his happiness or sink in the attempt. If you have any advice that may be of service in this exigence, let it be speedy for never had I more need of consolation.

Yours,

M. R.

P.S. Direct as your last under cover to the Nuncio, that man is faithful; but, beware of Seaton ... He has a brother in the service of the Hamiltons, I more than fear he has already betrayed some things to your prejudice. My uncle of Corocin contributes to my persecution by proposing an alliance with the house of Austria: the bearer will inform you at full the contents of this letter. Farewell, pity me and continue to love me!

This next letter was written after Mary's marriage to Darnley on 29 July 1565.

Letter 4:

Mary to Lord Bothwell

Cruel as your approaches are, I pardon them; but oh, too little sensible of the pangs I feel, you ought rather to have applied balsams than corrosives to wounds like mine! 'Tis true I am married and have given myself to another, and in that act have set aside the oft repeated promise I made you; but were self-interests forgot and impartial justice had liberty to speak, you would, with the softest compassion, reflect on the sad necessity that forced me to it! France, Spain, England and Rome were providing me husbands; Murray was depriving me of everything but the name of queen! How, but by marriage, could I put a stop to the solicitations of the one side, or have curbed the insolence of the other? Well you know, it was not in my power to make choice of you, without I could have been content not only to see my crown torn from me, but also resign both our lives to glut the implacable malice of our foes! You tell me Lord Darnley is handsome and well made! Ungenerous Bothwell; well are you convinced I have no eyes for any charms but yours! What induced me to make choice of him rather than any other, was because I would avoid giving any umbrage to the contending princes, whose equal pretensions might have expected equal favours; but in this marriage, which in the world's eye will seem wholly induced by inclination, neither Rome, nor France, nor Spain can be disobliged; nor can Elizabeth with any show of justice blame me; because it was on her recommendation I first consented to listen to his suit: and in preferring him to Leicester, I cannot but have the approbation of the whole judging world! Think not that it was love that furnished me with arguments to justify my choice; for I protest by the same dread power, by which I have so often sworn, that Bothwell was the dearest thing on Earth, that he is still so, and ever will be so, while I have life;

and Darnley ... but the property of my revenge on Murray! Oh, Bothwell, did you but know what unparalleled tyranny I was treated with by that assuming traitor, you would not wonder I had recourse for shelter to the expedient. The haughty arrogance of both he and Hamilton is now reduced to low submissions, and though they murmur they dare not complain! Depend on this truth, that nothing less than what I have done could have secured the life of Bothwell.

The cruel and designing Murray had irretrievably made you the sacrifice of his ambition, and I think it needless to say, that motive was sufficient and perhaps the most weighty of any to influence me to this action; that, by making my person the victim of one's, I might preserve the more dearer part of me from falling one to the other's more destructive passion! The first step I took was to inspire the new made king with notions to your advantage. By the time this reaches you, you will receive an order to return to court, where you will be encouraged and promoted. I shall see you, my dear Bothwell, though not as I could wish, yet I shall see you in safety, and while Heaven permits that blessing to me, I never can be truly miserable,

M. R.

This next letter was written sometime after the murder of Mary's secretary, David Rizzio, in March 1566, and before the birth of her son, James, in June that same year.

Letter 5:

Mary to Lord Bothwell

With a difficulty not to be imagined, not to be expressed, do I get an opportunity of writing this. My bodily indisposition, joined to the troubles of my mind, render me incapable of invention. I suffer myself to endure the eternal presence of the persons I most hate, rather than be at the pains of making an excuse to be alone. That spirit, that courage that was used to bear me through the greatest fatigues is now evaporated and extinct. A laziness of soul possesses me. I cannot think, I cannot resolve on anything. Assist me in this perplexity, my dear Bothwell!

Advise me, comfort me, find some way for my relief! I have no friend but you, and sure, if you are such, you will not suffer me long to bear these insults. But what is it I am asking? 'Tis dangerous to be loyal! Poor Rizzio! Only because he loved his queen, fell a sacrifice to this injurious husband! My life is next – nor am I spared but for the sake of the unborn heir of empire. Delivered once of that dear burden, my business in this world is done, and Darnley will reign alone. I know that my death alone can gratify the ambition of that ungrateful man; or the unceasing malice of the English queen. Yet might a way be found to snatch me from the impending ruin, had anyone the boldness to attempt it. Murray, all stern and fierce as he is by nature, expresses a concern for my ill treatment, and seems to hint at some design on foot for recovering that prerogative I so unadvisedly gave up.

But he, alas, has been so sullen already – so arbitrary and insulting when in power, I dread to invest him with the same again – I fear it would be exchanging one misfortune for another. If he should communicate any of his intentions to you, answer him with caution. If he could be sincere, I know he has the means to serve me – fathom him, if possible, and let me know your opinion directed under cover to Lady Lusse [a close relative of Bothwell's mother and a confidante of Mary].

The Bishop of Ross informs me that Morton [James Douglas, Earl of Morton] is returning from the North; if so, I may believe that Murray's working brain has not been idle – but whether for mine or his interest, Heaven only can resolve. Keep a fair correspondence with him, however, till we see the issue, which a little time will soon determine ... Farewell, keep me ever in your thoughts,

M. R.

P.S. Since I wrote this, Murray has been to visit me, and finding me all bathed in tears, the daily tribute that my griefs exact, bade me be of good comfort, for a blow would soon be given, that would restore all things to their proper order. I know not what he means, unless it be the death of the king, nor had I time to ask. Hamilton came in and broke off our conversation. I wish you would inform yourself and me with all convenient speed, but do it in a manner he may not think I am concerned in the enquiry. Once more adieu, my ever, dear Bothwell. Pity me, pray for me and never cease to love me.

Letter 6:

Mary to Lord Bothwell (c. late 1566 or early 1567)

That I answered yours no sooner was owing to the struggle in my mind occasioned by proposals so shocking to a woman of my gentle nature. Heaven knows I love not blood, and the thought of having that of a husband is terrible to reflection; yet self-preservation is the first of laws, and if there remain no other means, I must submit to this. I could wish either that Murray was not engaged in the design, or that he did not know I was acquainted with it. You, my dear Bothwell, are too liable to give credit to hate him. Who knows what use he may hereafter make of the guilt he makes me to become a sharer in? But it is now past remedy, and I must make a show of confidence. Never was a soul more hurried than mine has been this dreadful night! A thousand horrible ideas have run through my distracted brain; sometimes I thought I saw the king all covered over with wounds, and with his dying breath imploring vengeance on his inhuman murderers! At others, wild imagination presented the conspiracy unravelled, and Morton, yourself and Murray, already fallen victims of his revenge; while he, exulting in his cruelty, held a drawn dagger at my breast! Oh, what variety of horrors has this design involved me in! Why was I endowed with a soul so little capable of cruelty, yet urged to acts that have so much the appearance of it? I never loved this Darnley, and his ingratitude has made me hate him. Yet could I with pleasure part with some of my blood to ransom his, were there a possibility of avoiding it. How am I then guilty? 'Tis he himself that brings on his own fate. He forces me, he drives me to this abhorred extremity; and his must be the blame. Oh, that I could always retain this thought! That I could wholly banish a softness prejudicial to my peace!

But 'twill not be, in spite of all my efforts, and all my monstrous wrongs. Pity returns, and overwhelms my soul! Cure me of this weakness, and inspire me with notions suitable to the enterprise in hand; the very idea will otherwise distract me, and in the moment of the execution, I shall cry out, Forbear! And all betray! Exert, then, my dear Bothwell, that all-prevailing wit and eloquence of yours to furnish me with arguments to overcome so unseasonable tenderness. 'Tis in your power to make me almost anything. Represent the injuries I have received from this tyrannical husband, the vast indignities, the dangers that nothing but his death can free me from; but above all, make me remember, that while he lives I am deprived of the power to make my Bothwell happy. That last remonstrance, perhaps, may arm my feeble resolution, and while that glorious image is in view, I could, methinks, with unrelenting hands, myself perform that deed. I expect a letter from you this night, with a further account of the whole plan of the design, which, while in agitation, will never suffer me to know a moment's peace. Afford me all the satisfaction you are able in this tempest of my divided thoughts, and know, what I do, I do for you,

    M. R.

This next letter was written shortly after Darnley's murder on 10 February 1567.

Letter 7:

Mary to Lord Bothwell

By Darnley's death I am indeed once more a queen, again enjoy those pleasures that power affords, and have the means of punishing and rewarding indifferent persons, and in trifling causes, yet am still circumscribed. The more material business of my life remains unfinished. I am a queen, but you are not a king; till I accomplish that, the work is not complete, nor can I taste the sweets of royalty.

I begin to think Murray at last sincere, and approve of your design in engaging him to favour your divorce, which the bishop seems to make a light matter of, but I am afraid will not be so easily attained as he or you may imagine.

The apology you make for your long stay at Dumbarton is altogether needless. I am so far from resenting it, that I look on this self-denial as the most prudent thing you ever did. There are at this time many eyes upon our actions, and to be too frequently seen together at present might be a means of preventing of our being forever together hereafter. Send me a copy of what you write to Murray, enclosed in your next, and if possible make an interest with Lansford, in whose power it is to be serviceable to you on this account. Let my secretary know what sums are wanting to carry it on, and they shall be remitted to you. Morton and some others attend to speak with me, and I have time to say no more, but that I am ever, my dear Bothwell,

M. R.

P.S. The Bishop of Ross intends you a long letter of instruction, which I would have you observe in everything. You have not a better, or a more sincere friend on Earth.

The next letter was written shortly after Bothwell had been granted a divorce from his wife, Lady Jean Gordon.

Letter 8:
Mary to Lord Bothwell (c. 11 May 1567)
Fortune, grown weary of persecuting me, at length grows as extravagant in her blessings as she was in the former part of

my life in her cruelty; and your divorce being looked upon as good as completed, Murray himself proposed you to me as a husband, nay seemed eager in his pressures that I would give him my promise that you should become so immediately you were in condition.

Scarce could I contain the joy of my exulting soul – scarce keep my tongue from letting him know how much my heart took part in his persuasions. Never did I so much as then assume the politician. Had any other discoursed to me in the manner, sure I am I had not been able to conceal the pleasure it gave me! But the often experienced falsehood of that earl secured my caution, and made me reply no otherwise than that I would be advised by him in everything. 'Tis possible that he may in this be cordial; but to apprehend the worst is certainly the most safe. He cannot, however, recede from what he has said, and Morton, and several others, have of late spoke of you with that respect, that I am sensible he has communicated to them his intentions of uniting us.

Though I know you are to be in Edinburgh in so short a time, I could not delay making you the partaker of those transports you are the author of. There is a delicacy in such a love as mine, which will not suffer me to be blessed alone, and when I think this happy news has reached you, I shall indulge myself in sympathy with those ecstasies that I flatter myself you will feel at the receipt of so unexpected

an information. Make all the convenient speed you can to
town; I now long with double impatience for your presence;
it is not Bothwell, a man whose freedom with me love alone
could authorise, but my intended husband and future king
that I shall now embrace. Haste then to the arms, though
ever present to the heart, of

M. R.

Letter 9:
Mary to Lord Bothwell (May 1567)

I write to you with infinitely more tranquillity of mind than
that with which my last letter was dictated. Murray has well
retrieved his character, and more contributed to my felicity
than heretofore to my vexation. The Bishop of Orkney,
from whom I least expected it, is wholly on our side; and
'tis the earl to whom we are indebted for this change in his
behaviour: I put myself among the obliged, because I am
really so, though they who serve me most believe at the same
time they are acting the reverse of my inclinations. See by
this how very necessary dissimulation is. My very enemies,
by imagining they undo me, make the happiness of my life;
and those who wish to see me most wretched, unite to make
me most completely blest! Did Morton, Orkney and the
rest of that turbulent faction know the perfect attachment
we have to each other, would they plot to join us? No! They
would sever us forever! Thus, by a concealment of our

mutual tenderness, do we disappoint all the strategems that would otherwise be formed to the ruin of it, and triumph in security. I expect not to hear from you anymore, neither do I desire it. The great design grows now so near the point of being executed, that I would have your thoughts wholly taken up with managing to the best advantage this last and only trial of our fortune. I am now of the opinion that it cannot fail, and feed my fond imagination with a thousand glorious ideas of your approaching greatness! It will be a joy unspeakable to see you on the Scottish throne; but, to reflect you are seated there by me, a pride and pleasure that it is not in language to represent, and can only be reached by thought.

Oh, my Bothwell, my heart beats high with expectation, and every faculty of my soul is on fire with the impatient hope. 'Tis but three days before the grand catastrophe arrives, yet do they seem so many ages! Be you more cool to attend the longed for issue, or you will be little able to carry on the charge entrusted to your care, and on which depends not only our lives, but fortune and fame! Indulge in secret the swelling rapture; but let no outward sign of joy appear, till you are past prevention in the arms of

M. R.

James I of England (and IV of Scotland)
and Anne of Denmark

James Charles Stuart was born on 19 June 1566 at Edinburgh Castle in Scotland, the offspring of the ill-fated marriage between Mary, Queen of Scots and Lord Darnley. He became king of Scotland when a little over one year old, after his mother was forced to abdicate. For the next eleven years, a series of regents ruled the country. With Protestantism in the ascendency in Scotland, James was raised in that faith and not according to the Roman Catholic traditions of his mother, whom he never saw again after her imprisonment and exile when he was still an infant.

The young king was an accomplished intellect, if a troubled soul – hardly surprising given that his deposed mother was accused of involvement in his father's death, and that James was for much of his childhood a puppet of the regents. However, in October 1579 he was formally recognised as of an age to rule. Around this time, he fell under the influence of a French nobleman and cousin of his father who had recently arrived in Scotland – Esmé Stewart, Sieur d'Aubigny. Stewart became James's favourite, who made him Duke of Lennox (the only man to possess a ducal title north of the border). James was known for a string of male favourites – among them George Villiers, the son of an untitled squire. While historians continue to debate the exact nature of the king's relationships with several of his favourites, it is clear that he grew enormously emotionally attached. Some suggest that these associations were akin to fraternal or paternal relationships, while others – both then and now – suspect that he had a number of male lovers.

Regardless, in his early twenties James did what was expected of him and took a bride. In 1589 he married Anne of Denmark, daughter of King Frederick II, in a proxy ceremony in Copenhagen. She was fourteen at the time, and the pair seem to have enjoyed each other's company initially. When Anne set sail from Norway to Scotland after the marriage ceremony, she was caught in raging storms and was forced to turn back. James was apparently so concerned for her safety that he went out to join her in Scandinavia, where they undertook another wedding ceremony in person before finally returning to Scotland in May 1590.

But this initial tenderness and concern soon gave way to tension and discord, not least when James placed their first-born child, Henry (b. 1594), in the custody of the Earl of Mar at Sterling Castle – just as James himself had been under the Mars' care as an infant. Anne – who would have seven children with James, three of whom survived to adulthood – could not bear the parting and was suspicious of Mar's influence. There was also marital upset in the aftermath of the Gowrie conspiracy in 1600, when the Earl of Gowrie, John Ruthven, and his brother Alexander were killed after an apparent attempt to attack the king. Anne counted two Ruthven sisters among her household and demanded their reinstatement after James dismissed them. James was also much displeased at Anne's conversion to Catholicism, a move that sparked political unrest. Meanwhile, Anne was tiring of her husband's excesses, notably his drinking, while in 1613 she accidentally shot and killed his dog on a hunting expedition, sparking another falling out. The previous year, Henry, Prince of Wales, had died of typhoid fever aged just eighteen and it was perhaps this incident above all others that marked the inexorable drift between king and queen.

James had added the English Crown to that of Scotland following the death of Elizabeth I in 1603. After that time, the couple moved their court to England. Anne took to life in the capital, while James preferred a base away from the hubbub of London. While highly capable in certain respects (he wrote well-received works on subjects as diverse as witchcraft and the nature of kingship), he lacked the attention to detail required of truly great leaders and was prone to misjudgement. Henry IV of France would famously say of him that he was 'the wisest fool in Christendom'.

James inherited an England mired in debt and was unable to forge a close relationship with Parliament, in large part because of concerns over his consistent demand to be allowed to unite the English and Scottish governments and reign as king of Great Britain. Conspiracies against him became a hallmark of his reign, most notably the Gunpowder Plot of 1605, when disaffected Catholics planned to blow up the king and his ministers at the opening of Parliament. James briefly enjoyed an upswing in his dealings with Parliament in the aftermath of the plot, but normal service would soon resume. Relations had deteriorated to such an extent by 1614 that he spent the next seven years ruling without a parliament at all.

Both James and Anne suffered from ill health in their final years. She died in 1619 of dropsy, separated in all but name from her husband. He, meanwhile, spent much of the 1620s away from his power base in London – his son and heir, Charles, already filling the vacuum – drinking excessively and fending off a string of ailments until dysentery claimed him in March 1625.

The Letters

The following letters (Anne's both from 1603, and James's likely the same year) open a window on to a relationship that was well past the first bloom of infatuation but was yet to reach the mutual discontent and malaise for which it was destined. There is evident anger towards her husband in Anne's second letter, written after a fight had broken out between English and Scottish nobles at Windsor over a matter of etiquette. She had personally intervened to put the combatants under guard, a move James considered hasty and unhelpful. News then reached Anne that one of the pugilists had subsequently been welcomed into the company of the king, a fact that infuriated her. But in the first note here, there is plentiful evidence of a playfulness between the couple, even after some fourteen years of marriage. Meanwhile, James touches on the vexed subject of their son Henry residing with the Earl of Mar. Even as passions run evidently high, he expresses apparently sincere love for his queen.

Letter 1:

Anne to James (1603; written after his accession to the English throne)

My Heart,

I am glad that Haddington [Thomas Hamilton, Earl of Haddington] hath told me of Your Majesty's good health, which I wish to continue. As for the blame you charge me with of lazy writing, I think it rather rests on yourself, because you are as slow in writing as myself. I can write of no mirth but of practice of tilting, of riding, of drumming, and of music, which is all, wherewith I am not a little pleased.

So wishing Your Majesty perpetual happiness, I kiss Your Majesty's hand, and rest.

Your Anna, R.

Letter 2:

Anne to James (1603, after the drama at Windsor)

Sir,

What I have said to Sir Roger [Aston; a courtier and favourite of James] is true; I could not but think it strange that any about Your Majesty durst presume to bring near where Your Majesty is, one that had offered me such a public scorn, for honour goes before life, I must ever think. So humbly kissing Your Majesty's hand, I rest ever yours,

Anna, R.

Letter 3:

James to Anne (1603)

My Heart – Immediately before the receipt of your letter, I was purposed to have written unto you, and that without any great occasion, except for freeing myself at your hands from the imputation of severeness. But now your letter has given more matter to write, although I take small delight to meddle in so unpleasant a process. I wonder that neither your long knowledge of my nature nor my late earnest purgation unto you can cure you of that rooted error that any living dare speak or inform me in any ways to your prejudice; or yet that you can think them your unfriends who are true servants to me.

I can say no more; but protest, upon the peril of my salvation and damnation, that neither the Earl of Mar, nor any flesh living ever informed me that you were upon any popish or Spanish course, or that you had any other thoughts but a wrong-conceived opinion that he had more interest in your son, or would not deliver him unto you; neither does he farther charge the nobleman that was with you there; but that he was informed that some of them thought by force to have assisted you in taking my son out of his hands; but as for any other papist or foreign practice, by God! He doth not so much as allege it. Therefore, he says he will never presume to accuse them, since it may happen well to import you offence; and therefore I say over again leave these forward, womanly apprehensions; for I thank God I carry that love and respect unto you, which, by the law of God and Nature, I ought to do to my wife and mother of my children; but not for that you are a king's daughter; for, whether you were a king's or a cook's daughter, you must be all alike to me, being once my wife. For the respect of your honourable birth and descent I married you; but the love and respect I now bear you is because that you are my married wife; and so, partaker of my honour as of my other fortunes. I beseech you, excuse my rude plainness in this; for, casting up of your birth is a needless impertinent argument to me. God is my witness,

I ever preferred you to all my bairns, much more than to any subject; but, if you will ever give place to the reports of every flattering sycophant who will persuade you that, when I account well of an honest and wise servant for his true, faithful service to me, that it is to compare or prefer him to you, then will neither you nor I ever be at rest or peace.

I have, according to my promise, copied so much of that plot (whereof I wrote unto you in my last) as did concern my son and you; which herein is enclosed, that you may see I wrote it not without cause; but I desire not to have any secretaries than yourself. As for your dool [grief] made concerning it, it is utterly impertinent at this time, for such reasons as the bearer will show unto you, whom I have likewise commanded to impart diverse other points unto you; which, for fear of wearying your eyes with any rugged hand, I have herein omitted, praying God, my heart, to preserve you and all the bairns, and send me a blithe meeting with you, and a couple of them.

Your own,

James R.

To finish, four letters between James and George Villiers, who is widely thought to have become James's lover in around 1614. To the shock of many courtiers, the pair were demonstratively affectionate to each other in public, despite James's various proclamations against homosexuality. The king even-

tually made Villiers the Duke of Buckingham. In response to concerns from the Privy Council about favouritism, James responded: 'I, James, am neither a god nor an angel, but a man like any other. Therefore I act like a man and confess to loving those dear to me more than other men. You may be sure that I love the Earl of Buckingham more than anyone else, and more than you who are here assembled. I wish to speak in my own behalf and not to have it thought to be a defect, for Jesus Christ did the same, and therefore I cannot be blamed. Christ had his John, and I have my George.' Villiers would remain an influential player in national life under Charles I, after James's death, until he was assassinated in 1628 by a disaffected army officer. These letters show, if nothing else, an extraordinary intensity of feeling for Villiers by the king. Note, James sometimes affectionately referred to him as Steenie, which probably derives from the description in the biblical Book of Acts of St Stephen having 'the face of an angel'.

Letter 1:

James to George (17 May 1620, the day after George's marriage to Katherine Manners, daughter of the Earl of Rutland)

My only sweet and dear child,

Your dear dad sends you his blessing this morning and also to his daughter. The Lord of Heaven send you a sweet and blithe wakening, all kind of comfort in your sanctified bed, and bless the fruits thereof that I may have sweet bedchamber boys to play me with, and this is my daily prayer, sweet heart. When you rise, keep yourself from importunity of people that may trouble your mind, that at meeting I may see your white teeth shine upon me, and so bear me comfortable company in my journey. And so God bless you, hoping you will not forget to read over again my former letter.

James R.

Letter 2:

James to George (c. December 1622)

My only sweet and dear child,

I am now so miserable a coward, as I do nothing but weep and mourn; for I protest to God I rode this afternoon a great way in the park without speaking to anybody and the tears trickling down my cheeks, as now they do that I can scarcely see to write. But alas, what shall I do at our parting? The only small comfort I can have will be to pry in your defects with the eye of an enemy, and of every mote to make a mountain, and so harden my heart against your absence. But this little malice is like jealousy, proceeding from a sweet root; but in one point it overcomes it, for as it proceeds from love so it cannot but end in love. Sweet heart, be earnest with Kate to come and meet thee at Newhall [Buckingham's Essex home] within eight or ten days after this. Cast yourself to be here tomorrow, as near about two in the afternoon as you can, and come galloping hither. Remember your picture and suffer none of the Council to come here. For God's sake write not a word again and let no creature see this letter. The Lord of Heaven and Earth to bless you, and my sweet daughter, and my sweet little grandchild, and all your blessed family, and send you a happy return, both now and you knows when, to your dear dad and Christian gossip [here used in the sense of 'friend'].

James R.

Letter 3:

James to George (c. December 1623)

My only sweet and dear child,

Notwithstanding of your desiring me not to write yesterday, yet had I written in the evening if, at my coming out of the park, such a drowsiness had not come upon me as I was forced to set and sleep in my chair half an hour. And yet I cannot content myself without sending you this present, praying God that I may have a joyful and comfortable meeting with you and that we may make at this Christmas a new marriage ever to be kept hereafter; for, God so love me, as I desire only to live in this world for your sake, and that I had rather live banished in any part of the Earth with you than live a sorrowful widow's life without you. And so God bless you, my sweet child and wife, and grant that you may ever be a comfort to your dear dad and husband.

James R.

Letter 4:

George to James (undated)

Dear Dad and Gossip,

Though I have received three or four letters from you since I last wrote to you, yet, as Tom Badger says, I am not behind-hand with you; for I have made a hundred answers to them in my mind, yet none that could satisfy my mind, for kinder letters servant never received from master. And for great a king to descend so low, as to his humblest slave and servant to communicate himself in a style of such good fellowship, with expressions of more care than servants have of masters, than physicians have of their patients (which hath largely appeared to me in sickness and in health), of more tenderness than fathers have of children, of more friendship than between equals, of more affection than between lovers in the best kind, man and wife, what can I return? Nothing but silence, for if I speak, I must be saucy, and say thus, or short of what is due: my purveyor, my good fellow, my physician, my maker, my friend, my father, my all. I heartily and humbly thank you for all you do, and all I have ...

Your Majesty's most humble slave and dog,

Steenie

Charles I and Henrietta Maria

Born on 19 November 1600 at Dunfermline Palace, in Scotland, Charles Stuart was the son of Queen Anne of Denmark and James VI of Scotland (also James I of England from 1603). A sickly child, he did not become heir to the throne until the unexpected death of his brother, Henry, when Charles was 12 years old. He became king in 1625 and oversaw one of the most tumultuous periods in British history, which culminated in 1649, with his execution and the temporary abolishment of the monarchy.

Charles's life was significantly impacted by the religious conflicts that rent Britain and Europe apart in this period. Back in 1534, Henry VIII had broken with the papacy in Rome and established the Church of England in pursuit of divorce from Catherine of Aragon and marriage to Anne Boleyn. Yet while Charles found himself head of a Protestant Church, his personal faith veered too far towards Catholicism for the liking of many within his realm who feared that papal authority might be ushered in again via the back door.

On the Continent, meanwhile, the Thirty Years' War raged on as Europe's great powers fought for dominance. In the early 1620s, James I hit upon the idea of wedding his son to the Spanish princess Maria Anna. He hoped that such a union between Protestant England and Catholic Spain might pave the way for diplomats to negotiate a European peace. The plan, however, was an unmitigated disaster. The English parliament had no stomach to bring such a prominent Catholic into the British royal family and instead urged war with Spain. Both James I and Charles took umbrage at what they considered impertinent interference from Parliament, especially given that Charles believed in the divine right of kings to rule unimpeded. But when Charles travelled to Spain in 1623 for formal negotiations on the marriage, he found his potential bride cold and superior. Moreover, the Spanish at first demanded that Charles convert to Catholicism and then wanted guarantees as to religious freedoms in England that Parliament would never approve. Charles returned to England brideless and now intent on pursuing war with Spain.

The trip had not been a complete waste of time, though. While he did not have his expected Spanish wife-to-be, Charles did meet the love of his life in Paris en route to the talks: Henrietta Maria, the youngest daughter of Henry IV of France. The couple married on 1 May 1625, when the princess was still just fifteen years old. The wedding ceremony at Notre Dame, in Paris, saw the Duc de Chevreuse stand in for Charles, who remained in England, and it was some six weeks before Henrietta Maria joined her new husband. In England, there was uneasiness about the heir to the throne taking a Catholic bride and the early part of the couple's married life was rocky as a result. She refused to attend his coronation in February 1626 due to its Protestant nature, while he expelled many of her French household later in the year and even sanctioned an attack on French territory in 1627 to assist the Protestant Huguenots of La Rochelle. Only in 1628 with the death of the Duke of Buckingham – Charles's favourite, but a *persona non grata* to his queen – did the couple move into a happier phase of married life.

By that time, Charles was on a collision course with Parliament, which was reluctant to grant him the sums he demanded for his various overseas military exploits. The result was that he spent the 1630s effectively ruling without Parliament and raising funds through a series of taxes that were divisive and frequently at the very edge of legality. In 1639 there was an uprising in Scotland (known as the First Bishops' War) in response to attempts by Charles to impose various aspects of Anglicanism upon the Church north of the border. By 1640, he was so desperate for money to deal with the uprising and finance his court that he was forced to recall Parliament, which was in no mood for compromise. Soon there was rebellion in Ireland, too. Then, in 1642, the country

descended into a bloody civil war between the English Parliamentarian forces and Royalists loyal to the king. Charles was
forced from London, relocating to Oxford, while Henrietta
Maria moved back to France for prolonged periods. In 1646
Charles handed himself over to Scottish forces in the hope
of buying time to negotiate a peace with the Parliamentar-
ians. The Scots, though, made a deal to release him to his
enemies. In January 1649, Parliament (which now consisted
of members loyal to Oliver Cromwell and his New Model
Army), indicted Charles on charges of treason. He was tried,
by a court whose legitimacy he refused to acknowledge, and
was condemned to death on 26 January. He was beheaded
near the Palace of Whitehall before a large crowd four days
later. His last words: 'I shall go from a corruptible to an
incorruptible Crown, where no disturbance can be.'

Henrietta Maria lived a difficult and often impoverished
life in France until her son was restored to the Crown as
Charles II in 1660. She stayed in England for a while but
returned once more to her homeland, where she died in 1669.

The Letters

*The first four letters in this series give a glimpse of the blos-
soming romance between Charles and Henrietta Maria.
They were all seemingly written between the contracting*

of their marriage and their wedding day. It is worth remembering that Henrietta Maria was only aged fifteen at the time, while he was a decade older. Nonetheless, her responses to his passionate missives shows impressive poise and self-assurance – qualities, it turned out, she would need in abundance.

Letter 1:

Charles to Henrietta Maria (c. 1624)

I have not dared to take the liberty of testifying to you by a single line, the impatience with which my soul has been tortured during my long waiting for the happy arrangement of this treaty, until I received the good tidings; begging you to be assured that besides the renown of your virtues and perfections – which is everywhere spread abroad – my happiness has been completed by the honour I have already had of seeing your person, although unknown to you; which sight has completely satisfied me that the exterior of your person in no degree belies the lustre of your virtues. But I cannot, by writing, express the passion of my soul to have the honour of being esteemed yours ...

Letter 2:

Henrietta Maria to Charles (c. 1624)

Monsieur – The impatience that you show me you have had during the time the treaty was pending, the satisfaction that you tell me you have received on the news of what has been accomplished here, give me certain assurance of your good will towards me, as you represent it by your letter. The king my brother, the queen my mother being willing that I should receive these testimonies of your affection, I will only say that if that has not an assured foundation in all the good that it makes you imagine in me, at least you will find a readiness to show you that you will not oblige an ungrateful person, and that I am, and shall always be, your very humble and very affectionate servant. Henrietta Maria

Letter 3:

Charles to Henrietta Maria (date unknown)

Madame — Your favours have made me so bold as to beg you to do me the honour of accepting this little present, which my servant will give you from me. Although it is totally unworthy of you, yet I hope you will receive it in good part, as coming from him who will be very glad to risk his life in your service, wishing nothing more than to be honoured with your commands, and to have some opportunity of showing by deeds, how much I am, madam, yours ...

Letter 4:

Henrietta Maria to Charles (date unknown)

Monsieur — Not being able worthily enough to commend the presents you have been pleased to send nor to thank you for them, I refer myself to Mr. Cary to express to you the esteem I have for them; as how much I cherish the honour of your friendship, the continuance of which will always be as agreeable to me as the opportunities of showing you that I am, monsieur, your very humble and very obedient servant.

Henrietta Maria

Subsequent letters come from the time of the civil war. They reveal a queen determined to set her king on what she considers the right course, and one frequently infuriated by his failure to do as she suggests. High politics and survival have evidently come to take precedence over romance. There are numerous hints to the strains put upon their union by the war. In Letter 5, for instance, Charles refers to his mail being intercepted. The pair also resort to using a numerical code to hide the meaning of particularly sensitive information. Letter 7, meanwhile, attests to the difficulties of communication over long distances and especially when the air is thick with rumours and innuendo from third parties. By the time we get to letters 13 and 14, the queen is in Holland struggling to pawn some of her jewellery to raise funds for her husband. The emotional roller coaster of it all is no more evident than in Letter 16, where Henrietta Maria sways between desperation and sudden, determined hope – striking reading for those who know how the story ends.

Letter 5:

Charles to Henrietta Maria (13 February 1643)

Oxford

Dear Heart – I never till now knew the good of ignorance; for I did not know the danger that you were in by the storm, before I had certain assurances of your happy escape, we having had a pleasing false report of your safe landing at Newcastle, which your letter of the 19th January so confirmed us in, that we at least were not undeceived of that hope, till we knew certainly how great a danger you had passed, of which I shall not be out of apprehension until I may have the happiness of your company. For, indeed, I think it not the least of my misfortunes, that for my sake you have run so much hazard; in which you have expressed so much love to me that I confess it is impossible to repay by anything I can do, much less by words. But my heart being full of affection for you, admiration of you, and impatient passion of gratitude to you, I could not but say something, leaving the rest to be read by you out of your own noble heart.

The intercepting of my letter to you of the 23rd February has bred great discourse in several persons and of several kinds; as my saying I was persecuted for places is applied to all and only those that I name then to be suitors, whereas the truth is, I meant thereby the importunity of others whom at that time I had not time to name, as well as some then mentioned; I confess 174 and 133 are not guilty of that fault. Some find fault as too much kindness to you; you may vow from what constellation that comes but I assure such, that I want expression, not will, to do it ten times more to you on all occasions. Others press me as being brought upon the stage; but I answer that, having professed to have your advice, it will be a wrong to you to do anything before I had it. As for our treaty, leaving the particulars to this enclosed, I am confident you will be content with it, concerning any part in it; for all the soldiers are well pleased with what I have done, but expect no cessation of arms; for the lower House will have none without a disbanding, and I will not disband till all be agreed. Lastly, for our military affairs, I thank God that here and in the west they prosper well; as for the north, I refer you to 226—140 for information.

So daily expecting and praying for good news from you ...

Letter 6:

Charles to Henrietta Maria (1 January 1645)

Oxford

Dearest Heart — I receive it as a good augury thus to begin this new year, having newly received your letter of the 30th December, which I cannot stay to decipher, for not losing this opportunity, it likewise being a just excuse for this short account. This day I have despatched Digby's secretary, fully relating the state of our affairs. Therefore, I shall only now tell you that the rebels are engaged into an equal treat, without any of those disadvantages that might have been apprehended when Tom Elliott went hence; and that the distractions of London were never so great, or so likely to bring good effect as now; lastly, that assistance was never so needful, never so likely as now to do good to him who is eternally yours.

Letter 7:

Charles to Henrietta Maria (2 January 1645)

Oxford

Dear Heart — Having deciphered your letter, which I received yesterday, I was much surprised to find you blaming me for neglecting to write to you; for indeed I have often complained for want of, never missed any occasion of, sending to you; and, I assure you, never any despatch went from either of my secretaries, without one from me, when I knew of it.

As for my calling those at London a Parliament, I shall refer that to Digby for particular satisfaction; this in general: if there had been but two, besides myself, of my opinion, I had not done it; and the argument that prevailed with me was, that the calling did no ways acknowledge them to be a Parliament; upon which condition and construction I did it, and no other ways; and accordingly by it is registered in the council books, with the council's unanimous approbation.

But you will find it was by misfortune, not neglect, that you had not been advertised of it sooner.

As for the conclusion of your letter, it would much trouble me, if you did not know your desire granted before it was asked. Yet, I wonder not at it, since that which may bear a bad construction has been presented to you in the ugliest form; not having received the true reason and meaning of it. The fear of some such mischance made me more careful to give you a full account, by Tom Elliott, of the reasons of the D. of R. [Duke of Richmond] and E. of S. [Earl of Southampton] journey to London; which, if it comes soon enough, I am confident will free you from trouble. But, if you do not have the patience to forbear, judging harshly of my actions, before you hear the reasons for them from me, you may often be subject to be doubly vexed, first with slanders, then with having given too much ear unto them. To conclude, esteem me as you find me, constant to those grounds you left me without; and so, farewell, dear heart.

Letter 8:

Charles to Henrietta Maria (4 January 1645)

Oxford

Dear Heart — I desired you to take notice that with this year I begin to new number my letters, hoping to begin a year's course of good luck. I have heard of, but seen, no letters from you since Christmas Day; the reason is evident, for our intelligence with the Portugal agent is obstructed, so that I am not so confident as I was that any of my letters will come safe to you. But methinks if Card. Mazarin [Louis XIV's chief minister in France] were but half so kind to us as he professes to be, it would be no great difficulty to secure our weekly intelligence. And in earnest I desire you to put him to it, for besides that, if the effects of it succeed, it will be of great consequence to me, I shall very much judge of the reality of his intentions according to his answer in this. If Ashburnham [a devoted royalist supporter] complains to you of my wilfulness, I am sure it in this way that you will at least excuse, if not justify me in; but if you had seen a former paper (to which being but accessory I must not blame his judgement), you would have commended my choleric rejection of it, the aversion to which it is possible (though I will not confess it until you say so) might have made me too nice in this, of which I will say no more; but consider well that which I sent in the place of it, and then judge.

My great affairs are so much in expectation that, for the present, I can give you but little account of them, albeit yet in conjecture (as I believe) that the rebels will not admit of my personal treaty at London, and I hope well of having 2,000 foot and horse, out of my smaller garrisons. As for the Scots, we yet hear no news of them, neither concerning this treaty, nor of that which I have begun with David

Lesley [a prominent Parliamentarian commander]. And, lastly, that the Duke of York's [that is to say, Charles and Henrietta's second son, James, who would later reign as James II] journey is absolutely broken, both in respect of the loss of Hereford, as that the relief of Chester is yet but very doubtful. But upon this design, having commanded Sr. George Ratcliff [another loyal ally to Charles and previously a dedicated lieutenant of Strafford in Ireland before he was recalled to England and impeached by Parliament] to wait upon him, I desire your approbation that he may be sworn gentleman of his bedchamber, for which, tho' he be very fit, and I assure you that he is far from being a Puritan, and that it will be much for my son's good to have him settled about him, yet I would not have him sworn without your consent. So God bless you, sweetheart,

Charles R.

Letter 9:

Charles to Henrietta Maria (14 January 1645)

Dear Heart — Pooly came the 12th–22nd January to whose great despatch, though for some days I cannot give a full answer, I cannot but at this opportunity reply to something in your letter, not without relating to something of this discourse.

As I confess it is a misfortune, but deny it a fault, your not hearing oftener from me, so excuse me to deny it can be of so ill consequence as you mention, if their affections were so real as they make show of to you. For the difficulty of sending is known to all, and the numbers of each letter will show my diligence. And certainly there goes no great wit to find out ways of sending; wherefore, if any be neglected more, then our wits are faulty. But to imagine that it can enter into the thought of any flesh living, that anybody here should hide from you what is desired, that every one should know (excuse me to say it) is such a folly, that, I shall not believe any can think it, though he say it. And for my affection to you, it will not be the miscarrying of a letter or two that will call it in question. But take heed that these discourses be not rather the effects of the weariness of your company, than the true image of their thoughts. And of this, is not the proposal of your journey to Ireland a pretty instance? For seriously of itself I hold it one of the most extravagant propositions that I have heard; your giving ear to it being most assuredly only to express your love to me, and not your judgement in my affairs.

As for the business itself, I mean the peace of Ireland, to show the care I have had of it and the fruits I hope to receive from it, I have sent the last despatches that I have sent concerning it, earnestly desiring you to keep them to yourself. Only, you may in general let the queen-regent and the ministers there understand that I have offered my Irish subjects so good satisfaction that a peace will shortly ensue;

this I really believe. But for God's sake let none know the particulars of my despatches. I cannot but tell you that I am much beholden to the Portugal agent, and little to the French; it being by his means that I have sent thee all my letters, besides expresses, since I came hither, though I expected most from Sabran [the French ambassador in London].

I will not trouble you with repetitions of news, Digby's despatch being so full that I can add nothing. Yet I cannot but paraphrase a little upon that which he calls his superstitious observation. It is thus: nothing can be more evident than that Strafford's innocent blood has been one of the great causes of God's just judgements upon this nation by a furious civil war, both sides being hitherto almost equally punished, as being in a manner, equally guilty. [Strafford was the former Lord Deputy of Ireland and close advisor to Charles until Parliament called for his execution in 1641. Charles had signed his death warrant.] But now this last crying blood being totally theirs, I believe it is no presumption to hope hereafter that His hand of justice must be heavier upon them, and lighter upon us, looking now upon our cause, having passed by our faults.

Letter 10:

Charles to Henrietta Maria (30 January 1645)

Dear Heart – Sunday last I received three letters from you; one a duplicate of the 30th December, another of the

6th January and the last of the 14th January; and even now one Petit is come with a duplicate of the last; wherein, as I infinitely joy in the expressions of your confident love to me, so I must extremely wonder that any who pretend to be a friend to our cause (for I believe you would not mention any information from the other side) can invent such lies that you have had ill offices done to me by any; or that your care for my assistance has been the least suspected, it being so far from truth that the just contrary is true. For I protest to God, I never heard you spoken of but with the greatest expressions of estimation for your love of me, and particularly for your diligent care for my assistance. But I am confident it is a branch of that root of knavery that I am now digging at; and of this I have more than a bare suspicion. And, indeed, if I were to find fault with you, it should be for not taking so much call of your own health as of my assistance; at least, not giving me so often account of it as I desire; these three last making no mention of yourself.

Now, as for the treaty that begins this day, I desire you to be confident that I shall never make a peace by abandoning my friends, nor such a one as will not stand with my honour and safety, of which I will say no more, because, knowing your love, I am sure you must believe me, and make others likewise confident of me.

I send you herewith my directions to my commissioners; but how I came to make them myself, without any others,

Digby will tell you, with all the news as well concerning military as cabalistical matters. At this time I will say no more, but that I shall in all things truly show myself to be eternally yours.

The Portugal agent has made me two propositions: first, concerning the release of his master's brother, for which I shall have 50,000 crowns, if I can procure his liberty from the king of Spain; the other is, for a marriage betwixt my son Charles and his master's eldest daughter. For the first, I have freely undertaken to do what I can; and for the other, I will give such an answer as shall signify nothing.

I desire you not to give too much credit to Sabran's relations, nor much countenance to the fresh agents in Paris; the particular reasons you shall have by Pooly, whom I intend for my next messenger. In the last place, I recommend to you, the care of Jersey and Guernsey, it being impossible for us here to do much, though we were rich, being weak at sea.

Letter 11:

Charles to Henrietta Maria (25 February 1645)

Dear Heart — The expectation of an express from you, as I find by the 4th February, is very good news to me; as likewise that you are now well with my diligence in writing. As to our treaty, there is every day less hope than ever that it will produce a peace; but I will absolutely promise you, that if we have one, it shall be such as will invite your return; for I vow that without your company I can neither have peace nor comfort within myself. The limited days for treating with are now almost expired without the least agreement upon any one article; wherefore I have sent for enlargement of days, that the whole treaty may be laid open to the world. And I assure you, you needst not doubt the issue of this treaty; for my commissioners are so well chosen (though I say it) that they will neither be threatened nor disputed from the grounds I have given them, which (upon my word) is according to the little note you so well remember. And in this, not only their obedience, but their judgements concur.

I confess, in some respects you have reason to bid me beware of going too soon to London; for indeed some amongst us had greater mind that way than was fit, of which persuasion Percy is one of the chief, who is shortly like to see you; of whom, having said this, is enough to show you how he is to be trusted or believed by you concerning our proceedings here.

In short, there is little or no appearance but that this summer will be the hottest for war of any that hath been yet; and be confident, that in making peace I shall ever show my constancy in adhering to bishops and all our friends, and not forget to put a short period to this perpetual Parliament. But as you love me, let none persuade you to slacken your assistance for him who is eternally yours, C. R.

Letter 12:

Charles to Henrietta Maria (20 March 1645)

Oxford

Dear Heart — Upon Saturday last I wrote to you by Sabran (but this I believe may come as soon to you), and I have received yours of the 7th Monday last, which gave me great contentment, both in present and expectation (the quick message being likewise a welcome circumstance). And yet I cannot but find a fault of omission in most of your latter despatches, that being nothing in them concerning your health. For, though I confess that in this no news is good news, yet I am not so satisfied without a more perfect assurance; and I hope you will, by satisfying me, confess the justness of this my exception.

I am now full fraught with expectation (I pray God send me a good unloading), for I look for some blow of importance to be given about Taunton or Shrewsbury. And I am confidently assured of a considerable and sudden supply of men from Ireland, likewise the refractory horse (as the London rebels call them) may be reckoned in; for hey it is not known what fomentors they have, or whether they have none. If the latter there is the more hope of gaining them to me: howsoever, I doubt not but if they stand out, good use may be made of them. Of this I believe to give you a perfecter account – next week, having sent to try their pulses. Petit, came yesterday, but he, having at London thrust his despatches into the state ambassador's pocket, I have not received them; and I would not stay to lengthen this, in answer of them, nor give you half hopes of good western news; knowing of an opportunity of writing to you within these three or four days ... and so farewell, sweet heart.

P. S. – Yours of the 10th I have newly received, whereby I find that you much mistake me concerning Ireland; for I desire nothing more than a race there, and never forbade your commerce there, only I gave you warning of some Irish in France, whom I then thought and now know to be knaves.

Letter 13:

Henrietta Maria to Charles (17 March 1645)

The Hague

My Dear Heart – It was with no small joy that I received your letter by Ringfield, for I was in the greatest anxiety. I thank God that Charles is with you, and that I perceive your resolution and constancy continue. Assuredly, God will assist us, and whatever may be said to you, do not break your resolution, but follow it constantly and do not lose time.

As to what you write me, about making [William Cecil, Earl of] Salisbury treasurer, I would do nothing in it yet, but wait awhile longer, for, as to the sum of money, it is too small to be considerable, and you know that it is a bone that will make the dogs fight, and you may gain more by the dissension that there will be amongst them than by the profit of the money: for this reason, do not dispose of it. As to sending you that money, I will make all possible diligence, but I do not know where to send it to you. Therefore, when you come to York, if you find the country well affected, Hull must absolutely be had; if you cannot, you must go to Newcastle, and if you find that this is not safe, go to Berwick, for it is necessary to have a sea port, for reasons that I will send to inform you of, by express person, as soon as I shall know that you are at a sea port, and that Charles is there too, for it is necessary that this person should speak to you before you go into Scotland. I will send him in your own ships, which I still keep, expecting news from you, and by that same way, I will send you some money; only send me a warrant, under your hand, to give to [Admiral Sir John] Pennington, to transport, any person whom I shall appoint. You must leave the name of the person blank, and let me have it. Send to fetch James as soon as ever you can; I should also wish you to send for Essex and [Henry Rich, Earl of] Holland to come and serve you; if they refuse, take away their places and keep them vacant, unless you come to some contest; else restore them as they were, provided that they serve you. Do not pass tonnage and poundage any more, for it is against yourself.

I am labouring with confidence and hope to obtain satisfaction, although it be from a person not easy to bind down, but interests have great power. I had sent Clarke to

you, but the wind has been so contrary that I do not think
he has passed: which is the reason that by this way, I send
you copies of what I sent by him, which is about what must
be done to pawn our great collar, and touching my daughter;
I think the way that must be taken is for you to send a
command to Wharton, to get him to have a blank warrant
drawn up very secretly by Bridgeman, and that Wharton
himself should carry it to the keeper, with a letter from you,
and have it sealed before him, and as such you will send it me
with diligence; for otherwise we could do nothing, as you will
see by the letters of Boswell. Also send me a letter of warrant
for Boswell, by which you command him to give up the collar
to me, that if I see we can get nothing for it here, I may send
it to your uncle. Send the letter to me, to make use of as I
shall see fitting.

Be careful how you write in cipher, for I have been
driven well nigh mad in deciphering your letter. You
have added some blanks which I had not; and you have
not written it truly. Take good care I beg you, and put in
nothing that is not in my cipher. Once again I remind
you to take care of your pocket, and not let our cipher be
stolen. I am so weary with writing that I will say nothing
other than kind, for I am more so than I could write, and
I hope that my actions will show you it. If Pennington has
not a warrant under your hand to stay with me till I inform
him of your pleasure to the contrary, send me one, for I

understand they want to play him an ill trick about it. He is too simple a man. It is his fault.

Letter 14:
Henrietta Maria to Charles (May 1645)

My Dear Heart — After much trouble, we have at last procured some money, but only a little as yet, for the fears of the merchants are not yet entirely passed away. It was written from London, that I had carried off my jewels secretly, and against your wish, and that if money was lent me upon them, that would be no safety for them; so that all this time, when we were ready to conclude anything, our merchants always drew back. At last, it was necessary to show your power, signed under your own hand, about which I have written to you before, and immediately we concluded our business; I thought it better and safer to send it you as I do without noise, than for you to send different persons to fetch the money, for it will not be known that it will be for you, and as much, and as little at once, as you please. I thought this way more assured than to send it in specie [coins], for were you to change your place, the money of this country would not pass, and in money of England we could not get it. I have given up your pearl buttons, and my little chain has done you [good]. You cannot imagine how handsome the buttons were, when they were out of the gold, and strung into a chain, and many as large as my great chain. I assure you, that I gave them up with no small regret. Nobody would take them to pledge, but only to buy them. You may judge, when they know that we want money, how they keep their foot on our throat. I could not get for them more than half of what they are worth. I have six weeks time in which to redeem them at the same price. My great chain, and that cross that I had bought from the queen my mother is only pledged. With all these I could not get any more money than what I send you. I will send tomorrow to Antwerp, to pawn your ruby collar, for as to [that], in Holland, they will not have it. For the largest collar, I am waiting a reply from Denmark. Every day hopes are given me that those of Amsterdam will send me money.

This is all that concerns money: but if we put all our jewels in pledge, and consume them without doing anything, they would be lost, and we too; for we should have nothing left to help ourselves with, when we should need it. For this reason, lose no time; you have lost enough already. Take a good resolution and pursue it. Remember your own maxim, that it is better to follow out a bad resolution, than to change it so often. I have received your letters by the man already named – they have made me very sad, for you do not speak of giving up your magazine as lost. I must tell you again, that you see that if at first you had acted as you had resolved, it might have been gained at this time, and also, since you had once tried to get it, it was needful to go on; for to begin, then to stop, is your ruin – experience shows it you. It is not enough to declare yourself in writing; actions must afterwards be seen. It is true that your game is yet fair enough, but if you do not play it well, it will not, be gained. You must dare and as to Hull, if your magazine is not yet out of it, you must play Hotham some skilful trick, for otherwise, there is nothing to hope. As long as you do not declare yourself, you cannot judge of your power, for no one will dare to declare himself. And think too, that I am risking all we have left in the world to get money, and that, when that money fails, there is no more, and that when it will be needful to pay persons for fighting, there will be no more; therefore, time is precious. I am very glad that you have commanded [rest of note missing].

Letter 15:

Henrietta Maria to Charles (5 May 1645)

My Dear Heart – The wind having been contrary so that Sir Baladin has not been able to cross, and having received letters from you by Cochram, in which I see you are not certain of your voyage to Ireland, I wished to write you this line, Stelling sending what I had written before, and which I believe you will have already received also by another road. I will reply to your letter, where you say that if you can go to Ireland, and that the road by England is not safe, that you will go to Ireland by Scotland, which is a road that I apprehend extremely; for the troops who are going are entirely devoted to the Parliament, and they will hold you as a prisoner, if the Parliament please: thus you cannot join the army of the Catholics nor approach Dublin by that road; I think that by Wales would be the most sure, if that country is well affected. You can always raise men enough there for a regiment for your person, as was your design, and to leave thence you have a ship for Ireland, of which you can make use; and be assured [of] Stradlin, and also of him whom I have with me, and indeed those of the fleet, who are well affected, and make them come on some pretext. If you were assured that the troops who should go to Ireland are going very soon, and Scotland would remain without these persons who are not well affected to you, Scotland would be a good place for you to go to, but whilst these devils are there, there is no safety; and do you think that the Parliament having refused for you to go, that the troops will let you go? I am much afraid lest this affair of the militia spoil your design. I pray God that you may refuse it.

As to the man whom you ask for, I pray you send a warrant under your hand to Santerre, who commands the ship that is here, to await my orders; for the warrant he has is under the hand of Pennington, and at this time, that cannot serve him. Also a letter for the King of Denmark, only of ceremony, like that you gave me before, and send me a copy of it, to make use of, if it be necessary. If you have already done it, you must send it me again. Adieu, my dear heart. This 5th May.

To the King, my lord.

Letter 16:

Henrietta Maria to Charles (11 May 1645)

The Hague

My Dear Heart — I have received your letter by the post, with the message that the Parliament has sent you, which I think is pretty fair, since they believe they can have everything by speaking high words. As to your journey into Ireland, I say nothing about it, having written on this subject before; but as to the discourse you have had with Calpepper about Hull, I must say in truth, that to me it is a strange thing, that there is any one who can argue against that, and that you have not attempted to get it already; for the longer you wait, the worse it will be; and [can you] believe, that if there come a fleet to fetch away the arms, you will be able to hinder it? If, before that you do not get the place, the folly is so great, that I do not understand it.

Delays have always ruined you. As to your answer on the militia, I would believe that you will not consent to pass it for two years, as I understand you will be pressed to do, and that you will refuse it. But perhaps, it is already done; you are beginning again your old game of yielding everything. For my own consolation, however, I will hope the contrary, till I hear the decision; for I confess that if you do it, you ruin me in ruining yourself; and that, could I have believed it, I should never have quitted England; for my journey is rendered ridiculous by what you do, having broken all the resolutions that you and I had taken, except of going where you are, and that to do nothing. If you had been willing to cede the militia when I was in England, I could have satisfied the Parliament, as I said; but you have done in this, I am afraid, as you did in the affair of the bishops; for at one time you could have entered in an accommodation about that and you were obstinate that you would not, and after all you yielded it.

Meanwhile, I went out of England, contrary to everybody's opinion, in the confidence I had of what you would do, and I have made myself ridiculous; whereas, if you had done as you had resolved, it would have been seen that what you yielded all that time was only out of fear of danger to my person and from your affection to me, and not for want of resolution, and that I had been in the right to go away: whereas, hitherto there is ground for believing that it is a vagary or a folly; for as for staying in York, without doing anything, I might have done that.

Forgive me for writing all this to you: the truth is, that I see I shall be constrained by my misfortunes, to retire to some place where I can pray to God for you. I understand they are willing to give you tonnage and poundage [a revenue-raising mechanism] for three years. I repeat to you, that if you cannot have it as you ought, that is to say, in your own power to dispose of it, you pass a thing against yourself; you see it by experience, for all that has been hitherto done

with it, has been against you. As to what you write me,
concerning the 7,000 pieces, I will not fail to send them.

As to the espure [meaning unclear] of James, the man
to whom you have promised it; is Mr. —. He was a cornet of
Henry Percy's company, a gentleman of worth. I think, that
for the present, one in that place is enough. I send you this
man express, hoping that you will not have passed the Militia
Bill. If you have, I must think about retiring into a convent,
for you are no longer capable of protecting anyone not even
yourself. Adieu, my dear heart, The Hague, this 11th May.

As I was closing this letter, arrived Sir Louis Dives, who
has told me all that has passed at Hull. Do not lose courage,
and continue to act with resolution, for now is the time to
show that you will make good what you have undertaken, or
you are lost. You must have Hull, and if the man who is in it
does not submit, you have already declared him a traitor, you
must have him alive or dead; for this is no longer a mere play.
You must declare yourself; you have testified your gentleness
enough, you must show your justice. Go on boldly; God will
assist you. You see what you have got by not following your
first resolutions, when you declared those of the Parliament
traitors. Let that serve you as an example; do not delay longer
now in consultations, it is action that must do the work at
this hour – it is time. I have wished myself in the place of
James in Hull; I would have flung the rascal over the walls,
or he should have done the same thing to me.

As to money, Goring is gone to hasten it. He doubts not of having it in a week. I am in such haste to despatch this bearer that I will say no more, nor write to any one else in the world. Courage! I never felt so much: it is a good omen. You must go on boldly in case of need; the time is come, since I see that there is no hope of an accommodation. May heaven load you with as many benedictions as you have had afflictions, and may those who are the cause of your misfortunes, and those of your kingdom, perish under the load of their damnable intentions.

Letter 17:

Henrietta Maria to Charles (23 May/2 June 1645)

My Dear Heart — The Prince of Orange having given me seven horses all bred from Barbaries, both father and mother, I have thought that it would serve you better to use them yourself than for me to use them for your service. I send them to you, and beg you to compassionate the groom who brings them. He cannot stay here, not being able to live on what they give him. He was my daughter's servant. I am expecting tidings from you with great impatience. I am going to see the army today, and shall return the eve of Pentecost. Meanwhile, I have given orders for the two hundred officers that you ask for me in one of your letters; and as to an engineer, we have found a very good one. As soon as I shall receive an answer to my letter, which I sent you by Apsley, I will do as you may command me, for I shall find here all that is needful ready. I will not trouble you more, but remain, ever yours ...

There is a final sting in the tail of this chapter. Charles I did not have a large collection of mistresses to rival those of his monarchical close contemporaries (not least his own son, Charles II). Nonetheless, he did not do without dalliances. In 1647, while imprisoned at Carisbrooke Castle on the Isle of Wight, he began an affair with Jane Whorwood, the thirty-six-year-old step-daughter of a leading Scottish royalist. They corresponded in coded notes and the following sala-cious snippet was written sometime after April 1648.

Letter 18:
Charles to Jane Whorwood (c. 1648)

There is one way possible that you may get a swiving [slang for sexual congress] from me ... you must excuse my plain expressions ... you may be conveyed into the stool-room [lavatory] which is within my bedchamber while I am at dinner; by which means I shall have five hours to embrace and nip [further sexual slang] you.

Charles II, Catherine of Braganza
and His Mistresses

Charles Stuart was born to Charles I and Henrietta Maria at St James's Palace on 29 May 1630, instantly becoming heir to the throne. As a teenager, he fought with his father on campaign during the English Civil War – a conflict that, of course, ultimately resulted in the king's execution and the overthrow of the monarchy itself.

In fear of his safety, the younger Charles left the English mainland in 1646, moving variously to the Channel Islands, France and the Netherlands. While resident in The Hague he had the first notable love affair of his life, with Lucy Walter (the daughter of minor Welsh gentry). Although the relationship was short-lived, she bore him a son – the first of many children for the prince.

After his father's beheading, Charles kept up efforts to defeat the forces of Oliver Cromwell, but to no avail. Following decisive defeat at the Battle of Worcester in September 1651, Charles fled to France – a dramatic escape that involved him hiding in an oak tree as the enemy roamed close by.

Charles based himself close to Paris, his life in exile funded by his cousin, the French king, Louis XIV. With Cromwell having established a de facto military dictatorship in Britain, Charles's prospects looked bleak. However, when Cromwell died in 1658, his son and successor, Richard, proved comprehensively unfit for the job and resigned his post before the next year was out. In 1660, a new religiously and politically diverse Parliament was installed and, after Charles provided guarantees of broad religious freedom and promised not to persecute his father's former enemies (all, that is, except for those who had taken part in the execution of the king), Parliament invited him to return and claim the throne.

Charles processed triumphantly into London on 29 May 1660, his thirtieth birthday. Freed from the trauma of the bloody civil war and the oppressive Cromwellian regime, the country – or at least, those with sufficient wealth and privilege – embarked upon a period characterised by intemperance and pleasure-seeking. It was a collective gesture of good riddance to the suffering and puritanism that had so recently been endured, with Charles proudly its figurehead. Yet not even the racy poetry of the Earl of Rochester, nor the none-too-subtle innuendo of what became known as 'Restoration drama' could hold a candle to the king's personal life.

When he'd lived in exile with his mother in France, Henrietta Maria had been keen for Charles to make a suitable royal match, but he rejected a succession of European princesses. He seemingly had no desire to be shackled into a marriage just yet. Lucy Walter was superseded in his affections by perhaps the most famous of all his mistresses – Barbara Villiers, later to become the Countess of Castlemaine. A noted beauty, she was already married when she began a passionate affair with Charles around the time that he became king. Notorious for the influence she wielded over him and his court, she had perhaps five children by him. But he maintained many other lovers too – famously, he had an eye for ladies of the stage, notably Nell Gwyn, with whom he fathered another child. At the time that he was thick with Nell, he was also wooing Louise de Kéroualle, a daughter of the French aristocracy and a future Duchess of Portsmouth, as well as mother to another of his illegitimate children. Nell, though, did not take to her much, nicknaming her 'Squintabella' on account of a slight imperfection she had in one eye.

For a while, Charles's head was turned by a comely and virginal young woman called Frances Stewart, who ultimately eschewed his advances in favour of the Duke of Richmond, much to Charles's annoyance. But there were plenty of other women who took to the royal bed – he had further children with the actress Moll Davis (whose dinner was once laced with a laxative by Gwyn, intent that her love-rival's evening with the king would not be a comfortable one) as well as the more high-born Elizabeth Killigrew and Catherine Pegge. All of which is to mention nothing of a string of other mistresses who did not fall pregnant, among them several more members of the aristocracy and a niece of France's powerful chief minister, Cardinal Mazarin.

Amid all the philandering, Charles somehow managed to find the time to make a traditional royal marriage – one forged in the crucible of political pragmatism. His bride was Catherine of Braganza, daughter of Portugal's King John IV. At the time, Portugal was in conflict with Spain and looking for international allies. Charles, meanwhile, acquired not only a wife but also Tangier (in modern-day Morocco), the islands of Bombay (which would provide the basis for future British expansionism in India), as well as a hefty monetary dowry. Catherine made the journey from her homeland to Portsmouth in 1662, meeting her betrothed for the first time on 20 May, just a day before they were married.

Their life together was a curious one. Charles, as we have seen, was incapable of being faithful yet he was loyal to her in his own way. Meanwhile, the fact that she was a Catholic made her unpopular with large swathes of the British population. When she suffered three miscarriages and it became evident that Charles might not get the natural male heir so dear to monarchs of the time, many around him pressed for a divorce. Yet, he stood by her, insisting that she be treated with all the respect due to a king's wife. Meanwhile, matters of state carried on regardless. There was the Great Plague to deal with, and then the Great Fire of London, while religious frictions were always simmering just below the surface.

With the king intent on maintaining his marriage, Catherine's enemies redoubled their efforts to remove her by other means. Most notably, in 1678 she was caught up in the entirely fictitious 'Popish Plot' and accused of planning to murder her husband – allegations that saw her likely to face trial until Charles's personal intervention. Catherine was well aware of her husband's infidelity – and was pushed to the brink when Barbara Villiers was inserted into her household – but somehow the union stood the test of time.

Charles's reign was characterised, on the one hand, by a hedonist streak among the nation's elite, and on the other, by ongoing religious and political instability – the latter not helped by the absence of an undisputed heir. Moreover, ordinary people soon came to weary of the excesses of the ruling class. Nonetheless, Charles symbolised a restoration of some kind of order after the tumult of the 1640s and 1650s, up until his death (brought on by an apoplectic fit) at Whitehall Palace on 2 February 1685. As he lay dying, his mind turned to his lovers. He expressed regret for the treatment of his wife, then pleaded: 'Let not poor Nelly [Gwyn] starve.' But it was Louise, Duchess of Portsmouth, of whom he said 'I have always loved her and I die loving her.'

As for Catherine, she remained in London at Somerset House until finally returning to Portugal in 1692, where she served as regent in the occasional absences of her brother, Peter II. She died in Lisbon on New Year's Eve 1705.

The Letters

Despite his extensive list of lovers, few of Charles's love letters have made it down to us. The king perhaps valued discretion more than he appeared to. The following notes, though, give a glimpse into his complicated personal life. Firstly, a letter sent to his wife-to-be shortly after the contracting of their marriage – indicative, perhaps, of Charles's desire to put their union on a sound footing from the outset. Its tone is affectionate for a woman he does not yet know, but at the same time inevitably somewhat distant and 'official'. There then follows a lovelorn ballad he composed for Frances Stewart, one of those rare things – a potential paramour who eluded his advances. Finally, there is a short but passion-filled note to Louise de Kéroualle, a sanctuary of the romantic love that he did not truly have for his queen.

Letter 1:

Charles to Catherine (July 1661)

London

My Lady and my Wife,

Already, at my request, the good Count da Ponte [the Portuguese ambassador] has set off for Lisbon; for me, the signing of the marriage has been great happiness; and there is about to be dispatched at this time after him one of my servants, charged with what would appear necessary: whereby may be declared, on my part, the inexpressible joy of this felicitous conclusion, which, when received, will hasten the coming of Your Majesty.

I am going to make a short progress into some of my provinces; in the meantime, whilst I go from my most sovereign good, yet do I not complain as to whither I go, seeking in vain tranquillity in my restlessness, hoping to see the beloved person of Your Majesty in these kingdoms, already your own, and that with the same anxiety with which, after my long banishment, I desired to see myself within them, and my subjects, desiring also to behold me amongst them, having manifested their most ardent wishes for my return, well known to the world. The presence of Your Serenity, only wanting to unite us, under the protection of God, in health and content, I desire.

I have recommended to the queen, our lady and mother, the business of the Count da Ponte, who, I must here avow, has served me in what I regard as the greatest good in this world, which cannot be mine less than it is that of Your Majesty; likewise, not forgetting the good Richard Russell [a Roman Catholic bishop and another Portugal-based ambassador], who laboured on his part to the same end.

The very faithful husband of Your Majesty, whose hand he kisses.

Charles Rex

Letter 2:

A poem to Lady Frances Stewart (c. 1663)

I pass all my hours in a shady old grove,
But I live not the day when I see not my love;
I survey every walk now my Phyllis is gone,
And sigh when I think we were there all alone,
Oh, then 'tis I think there's no Hell
    Like loving too well.

But each shade and each conscious bower when I find
Where I once have been happy and she has been kind;
When I see the print left of her shape on the green,
And imagine the pleasure may yet come again;
Oh, then 'tis I think that no joys are above
The pleasures of love.

While alone to myself I repeat all her charms,

She I love may be locked in another man's arms,

She may laugh at my cares, and so false she may be,

To say all the kind things she before said to me!

Oh then 'tis, oh then, that I think there's no Hell

Like loving too well.

But when I consider the truth of her heart,

Such an innocent passion, so kind without art,

I fear I have wronged her, and hope she may be

So full of true love to be jealous of me.

Oh then 'tis I think that no joys are above

The pleasures of love.

Letter 3:

Charles to Louise de Kéroualle (1684)

I should do myself wrong if I told you that I love you better
than all the world besides, for that were making a comparison
where 'tis impossible to express the true passion and kindness
I have for my dearest dearest Fubs [an affectionate nickname
Charles had for Louise, meaning 'chubby' but perhaps better
understood in the sense of 'voluptuous'].

Mary II and William III (and II of Scotland)

Mary Stuart was born on 30 April 1662 at St James's Palace in London, the daughter of James II (and VII of Scotland) and Anne Hyde. At the time of her birth, her father was the Duke of York, while his brother reigned as Charles II. Although both her parents converted to Roman Catholicism, Mary was brought up a Protestant in accordance with the wishes of her uncle.

Mary's mother died while she was still a child, and her father remarried to Mary of Modena. From around the time of her mother's death, Princess Mary developed a keen attachment to Frances Apsley, the daughter of a courtier several years her senior. Apsley became the recipient of a large volume of highly impassioned, if juvenile, letters from the young Mary. Then, when she was about fifteen, Mary was promised in marriage to her Dutch cousin, William of Orange – the son of Charles II's sister. Charles himself was uncertain about the union, preferring instead an alliance with France, but he eventually became convinced of his political advantage and lobbied the Duke of

York to accept it. To begin with, Mary was appalled by the news, reputedly crying for two straight days.

The wedding ceremony was held on 4 November 1677 at St James's Palace, Mary once again succumbing to tears. She then travelled to the Netherlands with her new husband, enduring a turbulent sea crossing and dreadful weather, before they arrived in something like triumph at The Hague. Despite her understandable nervousness, she soon warmed to William and took to life in her new home. She was popular with the Dutch, while her marriage to a Protestant had also created good will in Britain. Still, life was not without significant challenges. William was often away on military business, which led some of those close to Mary to fear that he was neglecting her. She also suffered poor health and had a miscarriage in late 1675, with perhaps three more following in the years up to 1680.

After Charles II's death in 1685, Mary learned (while she was playing a game of cards) that her father had ascended to the throne and that she was next in the line for succession. She and William were instrumental in heading off a threatened bid for the Crown by Charles's illegitimate son, the Duke of Monmouth, who had previously been hosted by the couple when he lived in the Netherlands. However, having consolidated James's reign, they soon grew uncomfortable with his style of rule, particularly his willingness to govern by decree with a view to extending religious freedoms to non-Protestants. Relations only grew worse when he failed to provide support in defence of Orange when the forces of France's Catholic king, Louis XIV, invaded in 1672. James unsuccessfully attempted to drive a wedge between William and Mary by getting word to his daughter that her husband was having an affair with one of her ladies-in-waiting, Elizabeth Villiers. In truth, William probably was (although he was by no means a lothario by the standards of some other monarchs in this volume) and Mary probably knew it, but she took his denials at face value, and so her father's plan was scuppered.

By 1688, influential Protestants in Britain were growing increasingly concerned at what they considered James's pro-Catholic policies. When his wife gave birth to a son that year, there was deep concern that the heir to the throne was to be raised as a Catholic. There was even a wild conspiracy theory that Mary had endured a stillbirth and that another baby had been smuggled in to the royal chamber in a bedpan to be passed off as a legitimate heir, so guaranteeing a Catholic succession. At the end of June, a group of prominent nobles (known by history as the 'Immortal Seven') approached William with the idea that he and Mary should lead an invading army from the Netherlands to overthrow James.

William had harboured such a notion for some time. Mary, meanwhile, was devoted to following the will of her husband. Once she had made it clear that the pair might rule as equals (William did not much fancy playing second fiddle to Mary, who was higher up the line of succession than him), plans were accelerated for the incursion. William led an army that landed in November 1688, while Mary stayed in the Netherlands. James's forces were soon overpowered and he was allowed to flee to France before Christmas. Parliament declared his flight to be an abdication of the throne and bypassed his son to offer the crown to William and Mary as joint sovereigns. Mary joined her husband just after New Year 1689, and the couple processed into London before an adoring crowd (an experience bittersweet for Mary, who naturally felt sympathy for her father's predicament). The Glorious Revolution, as it became known, was complete.

In 1689, the Bill of Rights passed into law, establishing a balance between the powers of the Crown and Parliament. Not everyone was happy, though. From 1690, William spent a significant time in Ireland suppressing uprisings by Jacobites (the supporters of James), and he also had the French to deal with in the Netherlands. His campaigns in Ireland culminated in 1692 with victory at the Battle of the Boyne. In his absence, Mary ruled firmly (especially when it came to plots to return James to the throne) while striving to stay out of front-line politics as much as possible. Her reign, though, was not to be a long one. Having caught smallpox, she died on 28 December 1694. William was devastated, noting to one confidante that he was destined to be 'the miserablest creature on Earth'.

William was often absent from the country for the rest of his sole reign, and his popularity correspondingly declined. He died in 1702 after contracting pneumonia in the aftermath of a fall from a horse that had been seized from a Jacobite conspirator.

The Letters

The collection of notes that follow all date from 1690, when William was away on campaign in Ireland. They reveal a queen deeply attached to and concerned for her husband as he faces real and immediate peril. Although he would ultimately vanquish his enemy there, the strain upon Mary – forced to rule single-handedly back in London – must have been intense. The notes are imbued with a mix of both vulnerability and steadfastness.

Letter 1:
Mary to William (19 June 1690)
Whitehall
You will be weary of seeing every day a letter from me, it may be, yet being apt to flatter myself, I will hope you will be as willing to read as I to write. And indeed it is the only comfort I have in this world, besides that of trust in God. I have nothing to say to you at present that is worth writing,

and I think it unreasonable to trouble you with my grief, which I must continue while you are absent, though I trust every post to hear some good news or other from you. Therefore I shall make this very short, and only tell you I have got a swelled face, though not quite so bad yet, as it was in Holland five years ago. I believe it came by standing too much at the window when I took the waters. I cannot enough thank God for your being so well past the dangers of the sea; I beseech Him in His mercy still to preserve you so, and send us once more a happy meeting upon Earth. I long to hear again from you how the air of Ireland agrees with you, for I must own I am not without my fears for that, loving you so entirely as I do, and shall till death.

Letter 2:

Mary to William (22 June 1690)

Whitehall, half two at night

The news that is come tonight of the French fleet being upon the coast, makes it thought necessary to write to you both ways; and I, that you may see how matters stand in my heart, prepare a letter for each. I think Lord Torrington has made no haste. And I cannot tell whether his being sick, and staying for Lord Pembroke's regiment, will be a sufficient excuse. But I will not take up your time with my reasonings, I shall only tell you that I am so little afraid, that I begin to fear I have not sense enough to apprehend the danger. For whether it threatens Ireland, or this place, to me 'tis much at one, as to the fear; for as much a coward as you think me, I fear more for your dear person than my poor carcass. I know who is most necessary in the world. What I fear most at present is not hearing from you. Love me whatever happens, and be assured I am ever entirely yours till death.

Letter 3:

Mary to William (5 July 1690)

Whitehall

This is only to tell you I have received yours of the 28th, which puts me in many troubles that I shall not trouble you with at present. Tomorrow night an express shall go to you that cannot possibly be despatch'd tonight, and I am not sorry; for at this time I dare say but little by candlelight, and 'tis tomorrow the first Sunday of the month. I have really hardly had time to say my prayers, and was feign to run away to Kensington, where I had three hours of quiet, which was more than I have had together since I saw you. That place made me think how happy I was there when I had your dear company; but now ... I will say no more, for I shall hurt my own eyes, which I want more now than ever. Adieu; think of me, and love me as much as I shall you, who I love more than my life. I should have sent this last post; but not seeing Madame Nienhuys, hindered me then, and makes me send it you now, which I hope you excuse.

Letter 4:

Mary to William (6 July 1690)

Whitehall

I can never give God thanks enough as long as I live for your preservation; I hope in His mercy that this is a sign He preserves you to finish the work He has begun by you; but I hope it may be a warning to you, to let you see you are exposed to as many accidents as others; and though it has pleased God to keep you once in so visible a manner, yet you must forgive me if I tell you that I should think it a tempting God to venture again without a great necessity: I know what I say of this kind will be attributed to fear; I own I have a great deal for your dear person, yet I hope I am not unreasonable upon the subject, for I do trust in God, and He is pleased every day to confirm me more and more in the confidence I have in Him; yet my fears are not less, since I cannot tell, if it should be His will to suffer you to come to harm for our sins, and when that might happen: For though God is able, yet many times He punishes the sins of a nation as it seems good in His sight. Your writing me word how soon you hoped to send me good news, shows me how soon you thought there might be some action, and that thought put me in perpetual pain. This morning when I heard the express was come, before Lord Nottingham came up, I was taken with a trembling for fear that has hardly left me yet, and I really don't know what I do. Your letter came just before I went to chapel; and though the first thing Lord Nottingham told me was, that you were very well, yet the thoughts that you expose yourself thus to danger fright me out of my wits, and make me not able to keep my trouble to myself. But for God's sake let me beg you to take more care for the time to come; consider what depends upon your safety. There are so many more important things than myself, that I think I am not worthy naming among them. But it may be the worst will be over before this time, so that I will say no more. I did not answer your letter by the post last night, because the express could not be dispatched; and I believe more hindrances are come, for Lord Steward and Lord Pembroke write word they will be here tonight; but I can say very little upon the subject at present, for really I had my head and heart so full of you, I could mind nothing else.

It is now past 10 o'clock. I don't tell you for an excuse, for I am not sleepy; my impatience is too great to hear from you again, that I am not master of it, nor indeed of myself; so that you must excuse me from saying more than is just necessary ... I hope you will forgive me if I forget half what I have to say, for really my concern for you has got the mastery, and I am not able to think of anything else, but that I love you in more abundance than my own life.

Letter 5:

Mary to William (17 July 1690)

Whitehall

Every hour makes me more impatient to hear from you, and everything I hear stir, I think brings me a letter. I shall not go about to excuse myself; I know 'tis a folly to a great degree, to be so uneasy as I am at present, when I have no reason to apprehend any ill cause, but only might attribute your silence to your marching farther from Dublin, which makes the way longer. I have stay'd till I am almost asleep in hopes; but they are vain, and I must once more go to bed, and wish to be waked with a letter from you, which I shall at last get, I hope. Till I know whether you come or no, I cannot resolve to write you all that has passed this day, till which time I thought you had given me wrong characters of men, but now I see they answer my expectation of being as little of a mind as of a body. Adieu, do but love me, and I can bear anything.

Letter 6:

Mary to William (2 August 1690)

Whitehall

Unless I could express the joy I had at the thought of your coming, it will be in vain to undertake telling you of the disappointment 'tis to me that you do not come so soon. I begin to be in great pain lest you had been in the storm a Thursday night, which I am told was great ... I confess I deserve such a stop to my joy, since maybe it was too great, and I not thankful enough to God, and we all are apt to be too vain upon so quick a success. But I have mortification enough to think your dear person may be again exposed at the passage of the Shannon, as it was at that of the Boyne: This is what goes to my heart; but yet I see the reasons for it so good, that I will not murmur, for certainly your glory would be the greater to terminate the war this summer, and the people here much better pleased, than if they must furnish next year for the same thing again. Upon these considerations I ought to be satisfied, and I will endeavour as much as may be to submit to the will of God and your judgement; but you must forgive a poor wife, who loves you so dearly, if I can't do it with dry eyes; yet since it has pleased God so wonderfully to preserve you all your life, and so miraculously now, I need not doubt but He will still preserve you: yet let me beg you not to expose yourself unnecessarily, that will be too much tempting that Providence, which I hope will still watch over you ...

Letter 7:

Mary to William (9 August 1690)

Whitehall

I have had no letter from you since that of the 31st from Chapelford; what I suffer by it you cannot imagine. I don't say this by way of complaint, for I do believe you write as often as 'tis convenient or necessary, but yet I can't help being extremely desirous of hearing again from you. This passage of the river runs much in my mind, and gives me no quiet night nor day; I have a million of fears, which are caused by that which you can't be angry at, and if I were less sensible I should hate myself, though I wish I were not so fearful, and yet one can hardly go without t'other; but 'tis not reasonable I should torment you with any of this ... I have staid till I am ready to go to bed, and now can put off sealing my letter no longer. I pray God give me patience and submission; I want the first exceedingly, but I hope all is well, especially your dear self, who I love much better than life.

Letter 8:

Mary to William (19 August 1690)

Whitehall

Last night, when it was just a week since I had heard from you, I received yours of the 10th, after I was a-bed; I was extremely glad to find by it you had passed the Shannon, but cannot be without fears, since the enemies have still an army together, which, tho' it has once more run away from you, may yet grow desperate, for ought I know, and fight at last. These are things I can't help fearing; and as long as I have these fears, you may believe I can't be easy. Yet I must look over them, if it be possible, and force myself to talk, or presently everybody thinks all lost. This is no small part of my penance; but all must be endured as long as it pleases God, and I have still abundant cause to praise Him who has given you this new advantage. I pray God continue to bless you, and make us all thankful as we ought; but I must own the thoughts of your staying longer is very uneasy to me. God give me patience, I hope you will be so kind to write oftener. While you are away, it is really the only comfort this world affords, and if you knew what a joy it is to receive so kind a one as your last, you would by that, better than anything else, be able to judge of mine for you, and the belief that what you say upon that subject is true, is able to make me bear anything ... I need not repeat either how much I love you, nor how impatient I am to see you, you are kind enough to be persuaded of both, and I shall make it my endeavour, while I live, never to give you cause to change your opinion of me, no more than I shall my kindness to you, which is much above imagination.

*Catherine II ('the Great') of Russia
and Grigory Potemkin*

Catherine was in fact born Princess Sophie Friederike Auguste von Anhalt-Zerbst on 7 May 1729, in Stettin, Pomerania (then part of the kingdom of Prussia but now Szczecin in Poland). Her parents were Prince Christian August of Anhalt-Zerbst and Princess Johanna Elisabeth of Holstein-Gottorp. Although high born, at the time there was little to suggest that Sophie was destined to become the most powerful woman of her age, a figure to whom the monarchs of Europe would in due course bow.

Her fate, though, was sealed by a combination of her mother's fierce ambition and the desire of Prussia's leaders to forge closer ties with Russia at the expense of Austria. The key to her future was a second cousin, Peter – the son of Charles Frederick, Duke of Holstein-Gottorp, and Anna Petrovna, a daughter of Peter the Great. In 1742, Charles's childless aunt, Empress Elizabeth of Russia, chose Peter as her successor. She also began the search for a suitable bride for him. Her gaze fell upon the young Princess Sophie, who charmed Elizabeth sufficiently that she overlooked her disdain for Sophie's pushy and duplicitous mother, and picked her for his wife.

For Sophie, the betrothal was no source of joy. She had already spent time with Peter and found him charmless and unappealing. Nonetheless, she moved to Russia in 1744 and made great efforts to integrate. She sought to foster good relations with both her fiancé and the empress, devoted herself to learning the Russian language and was soon winning a name for herself among the population at large. In June that year, she converted to the Russian Orthodox faith (to the dismay of her Lutheran father) and received a new name – Yekaterina, or Catherine. On 21 August 1745, she and Peter were married in the Russian capital, St Petersburg. Peter had inherited the dukedom of Holstein-Gottorp on the death of his father a few years earlier, so the newlyweds set up home in Oranienbaum, Germany, where they oversaw the duchy and prepared themselves to eventually rule Russia.

The partnership, though, was not a happy one. Catherine had a sharp mind where Peter was emotionally and intellectually immature, prone to drunkenness and allegedly impotent (Catherine herself suggested the marriage was never consummated, although Peter eventually took a mistress so it is difficult to be sure on this point). Matters came to a head when the Empress Elizabeth died in

January 1762. Peter succeeded her as Emperor Peter III, with Catherine as empress consort, and they moved to St Petersburg. But his reign soon fell into crisis. The Russian Court quickly had its fears confirmed that Peter's sympathies lay rather more with Prussia, where he had grown up, than with the Russia that he now ruled. Catherine, on the other hand, had evolved into an exemplar of Russian nationalism.

With little love lost between husband and wife, she became the focal point of plots by leading figures in St Petersburg to unseat the emperor. In July 1762, just six months after Elizabeth's death, Catherine and her supporters executed an astonishing coup in which Peter was forced to abdicate and she took the throne in her own right. Within days of his deposition, Peter lay dead – whether murdered or by natural causes is still not known for certain.

Catherine would reign for thirty-four years, overseeing Russia's territorial expansion and implementing her own form of enlightened despotism – a mode of rule that combined autocracy with progressive social and economic policies inspired by Enlightenment philosophers such as her long-term correspondent, Voltaire. Over her lifetime, Catherine turned Russia into a true global player and became a cultural icon who continues to fascinate – a woman who succeeded at a time when it truly was a man's world.

Bound up with this fascination is a focus on her personal life. She inevitably made many enemies over the years and was subjected to countless scurrilous rumours centred around her sex. To this day, a vulgar myth persists about the nature of her death that is entirely without factual basis. What is true, though, is that Catherine did not adopt a virginal persona of the type preferred by Elizabeth I of England. Instead, she fully embraced her womanhood in all its aspects and did not hide or shy away from her sexuality.

There were, then, a plentiful number of lovers over the years. Among the first was a Russian officer, Sergei Saltykov, whom she would later claim was the true father – not Peter – of her son, Paul (who would go on to rule Russia after her death). She also had a daughter, Anna, in 1757 with a Polish nobleman Stanisław Poniatowski, although sadly the child died at fifteen-months old. Despite her affair with Poniatowski being relatively short-lived, Catherine would assist him in his election as king of Poland in 1764. Indeed, Catherine was famed for the beneficence she showed to various of her paramours, both when in a relationship with them and long afterwards, too.

Another of her lovers was Grigory Orlov, who fathered a child with her and whom she made a count. Orlov, son of a regional governor, was an artillery officer when he first caught the empress's attention and went on to play a pivotal role in the overthrow of Peter. For several years he was among the most powerful men in the country before a succession of missteps – and the actions of his rivals – saw his fall from grace. In order to win back Catherine's favours, he gifted her the famous Orlov diamond (roughly half the size of a chicken egg) but the pair split around 1772.

For a while, Orlov's place was taken by the aristocratic Alexander Vasilchikov but then, in 1774, she took up with her most famous lover of all, Grigory Potemkin – a man she once described as 'one of the greatest, the most comical and amusing, characters of this iron century'. He was an officer of the prestigious Horse Guards regiment and played a role in the coup against Peter. However, his relationship with Catherine was a slow-burn affair that did not bloom for another dozen years. By that time he was famous for his military exploits but was a divisive figure at court. Undoubtedly charismatic and enigmatic (he had long ago lost an eye in mysterious circumstances), he could also be big-headed and uncouth. Catherine came to greatly value his advice on political matters, though, and for a while he virtually held the status of emperor. Their personal relationship was intense and turbulent – he fell often into fits of jealousy and depression, while she constantly feared he would tire of her. In the end, the intensity became too much and their relationship as lovers fizzled out after a couple of years. Yet they remained political and spiritual soulmates. She rewarded him with all sorts of positions of power, while he was even allowed to vet future potential lovers for their suitability to her.

Chief among these later suitors was Platon Alexandrovich Zubov, who would become a prince of the Holy Roman Empire. He and Catherine became partners around 1789, when Catherine was sixty and he just twenty-two (Catherine developed a penchant for much younger men as the years rolled by). Despite initial scepticism from many observers, the pair stayed together until Catherine's death, from a stroke, in 1796. Yet Potemkin remains the dominant figure in the empress's romantic life. On his death from a sudden fever in 1791, she told a friend: 'A terrible deathblow has just fallen on my head ... my pupil, my friend, almost my idol, Prince Potemkin of Taurida [the Crimea], has died ... you cannot imagine how broken I am.'

The Letters

The following correspondence is between Catherine and Potemkin while they were lovers from 1774 until 1776. The translations are courtesy of Douglas Smith, who published a notable volume of their correspondence under the title Love & Conquest *(Northern Illinois University Press, 2004). The first note from Catherine is headed 'A Sincere Confession' and was written after she had recalled Potemkin to court with the intention of exploring their romantic potential. It is, in effect, a roll call and justification of her private life up*

*to that point, as well as a plea for she and Potemkin to give
their love a chance.*

Letter 1:

Catherine to Potemkin (21 February 1774)

A Sincere Confession

Maria Choglokova [a stewardess of the court whom
Empress Elizabeth asked to discover why Catherine and
Peter's marriage was childless] saw that after nine years
things remained the same as they'd been before the wedding,
and often having been scolded by the late empress for not
having tried to change them, she found no other means
than to have both parties choose freely from those persons
she had in mind. One party chose the widow Groot, who's
now married to Lieutenant-General of the Artillery Meller
[Groot was chosen with the idea of 'testing' Peter's fertility,
although the 'results' are unknown]; the other – Sergei
Saltykov, and him chiefly because of his obvious inclination
and Mama's [that is, Elizabeth's] persuasion, who'd been
driven to this by dire necessity.

Two years later Sergei Saltykov was sent away as an
envoy, for he had conducted himself indiscreetly and Maria
Choglokova no longer had enough power at the Great
Courts to retain him. After a year spent in great sorrow,
the present Polish king [Stanisław Poniatowski] arrived.
We took no notice of him, but good people, with their

empty suspicions, forced me to notice that he existed, that his eyes were of unparalleled beauty and that he directed them (though so near-sighted he doesn't see past his nose) more often in one direction than another. This one was both loving and loved from 1755 till 1761. But a three-year absence, that is from 1758, and the efforts of Prince Grigory Grigorievich [Orlov], whom again good people forced me to notice, changed my state of mind. This one would've remained for life had he himself not grown bored. I learned of this on the very day of his departure to the congress from Tsarskoe Selo [site of an imperial palace a few miles south of St Petersburg], and as a result I simply decided that I could no longer trust him. This thought cruelly tormented me and forced me, out of desperation, to make some sort of choice, one that grieved me then and still does now more than I can say, and especially at those moments when other people are usually happy. His every caress has aroused tears in me, so much so that I think I've never cried since my birth as I have this past year and a half. At first I thought I'd get used to it, but the further along, the worse it got; and as for the other Party [Peter], he began to pout, sometimes for three months at a time, and I must admit that I was never as happy as when he would get angry and leave me in peace, for his caresses only made me cry.

Then came a certain knight [that is, Potemkin]. Through his merits and customary kindness, this hero was

so charming that people, upon hearing of his arrival, were
already saying that he should take up residence here. But
what they didn't know was that we'd called him here, on the
quiet, with a note secretly intending, however, not to act
blindly upon his arrival, but to try to discover whether he
truly had the inclination which Briussha [Countess Praskovya
Aleksandrovna Bruce, a close friend of Catherine's] told me
many had long suspected he had, that is, that which I wanted
him to have.

Now, Sir Knight, after this confession may I hope to
receive absolution for my sins? You'll be pleased to see that
it wasn't fifteen, but a third as many: the first, chosen out of
necessity, and the fourth, out of desperation, cannot, in my
mind, be attributed to any frivolity. As to the other three,
if you look closely, God knows they weren't the result of
debauchery, for which I haven't the least inclination, and
had fate given me in my youth a husband whom I could've
loved, I would've remained true to him forever. The trouble
is that my heart is loath to be without love even for a single
hour. It's said that people try to conceal such vices under the
cloak of kindness, and it may be that such disposition of the
heart is more of a vice than a virtue. Perhaps it's wrong for
me to write this to you, for after reading it you might fall in
love with me or might not want to go off to the army fearing
that I shall forget you. But I really don't think I'd make such
a mistake, and if you want to keep me forever, then show me

as much friendship as love, and more than anything else, love me and tell me the truth.

The next few letters reflect a changeable relationship. Catherine sets aside the powerful persona reserved for her public life and reveals a part of herself that is playful, eager to please and sometimes plagued with self-doubt. The need to constantly 'prove' herself to Potemkin is striking, driven no doubt in part by his own insecurities, which are evident in his own letters and in her responses to them.

Letter 2:

Catherine to Potemkin (28 February 1774)

Grishenka [Catherine's pet-name for Potemkin, roughly equating to 'Little Pear'] isn't dear to me, he's more than dear. I slept well, but am very ill; my chest and head ache, and truly I don't know whether or not I shall go out today. But if I do, then it'll be because I love you more than you love me, which I can prove as easily as two and two make four. I'll go out just to see you. Few have as much control over themselves as you do. And what's more, few are so clever, so nice, so agreeable. I'm not surprised that the entire city has ascribed to you a countless number of women as your lovers. No one on Earth is better at busying himself with them, I suppose, than you. It seems to me there is nothing common about you, but that you

distinguish yourself greatly from others. I only ask you not
to do one thing: don't damage and don't even try to damage
my opinion of Prince Orlov, for I should consider that to be
ingratitude on your part. There's no one whom he praised
more to me and whom, quite evident to me, he loved more,
both in former times and now till your very arrival, than
you. And if he has his faults, then it is unfit for either you or
me to judge them and to make them known to others. He
loves you, and they are my friends, and I shan't part with
them. Now there's a lesson for you. If you're wise, you'll
heed it. It wouldn't be wise to contradict it since it's the
absolute truth.

In order for me to make sense, I must close my eyes
when I am with you or else I might truly say what I have
always laughed at: 'My gaze is captivated by you.' This is an
expression that I considered silly, improbable and unnatural,
but that I now see might be possible. My silly eyes will
become fixed watching you; not even an ounce of reason
can penetrate my mind and God knows how foolish I'm
becoming. If at all possible, I must not see you for three days
or so for my mind to calm down and to regain my senses,
otherwise you will soon tire of me, and rightly so. I am very,
very angry with myself today and gave myself a good scolding
and tried my hardest to be smarter. On the off-chance I
somehow actually get the strength and firmness, I shall take
a page from your book – the best example I have before me.

You are clever, you are firm and steadfast in the decisions
you have made, proof of which is that even for many years,
you say, you strove in our midst, and I did not notice, though
others told me.

Farewell, darling, about three days remain for our
rendezvous, for it will soon be the first week of Lent – days
of repentance and prayers when it will be impossible to see
you, since this would be bad in many ways. I must fast. Oh!
I can't imagine it and nearly cry from these thoughts alone.
Adieu, Monsieur, please write how you are today; pray, did you
sleep, well or not, and does your fever persist and is it high?
... How merry it would be if we could sit together and talk. If
we loved each other less, we'd be smarter, merrier. For even I
am a merry soul when my mind, and especially my heart, are
free. For you won't believe, my love, how important it is for
conversation that it not be excessively influenced by love.

Pray write whether you laughed upon reading this
letter, for I fairly roared with laughter while reading what
I'd written. What nonsense I've scribbled, the hottest fever
mixed with gibberish. Well, off it goes – perchance you too
will amuse yourself a little.

Letter 3:
Catherine to Potemkin (after 1 March 1774)

Sweetheart, what nonsense you spoke yesterday. Your
words still have me laughing even today. What happy

hours I spend with you. We spend some four hours together, and I'm not bored in the slightest and must always force myself, reluctantly, to part. My precious dear, I love you extraordinarily; you're nice, and clever, and merry and amusing, and I don't need the rest of the world when I'm sitting with you. Never in my life have I been as happy as I'm with you. I often wish to hide from you my inner feelings, but my heart usually blurts out its passion. It must be that it's full to the brim and so spills over. I didn't write to you the other day since I got up late and to your day's affairs.

Farewell, brother, behave cleverly around others so that no one can know what is or is not on our minds. I find a little dissembling terribly amusing.

Letter 4:

Catherine to Potemkin (after 19 March 1774)

No, Grishenka, it's quite impossible that my feelings for you will change.

Be fair with yourself: could I love someone after you? I think there's no one like you, and I don't give a damn about everyone else ... And there's still more I shall say to you: I don't like change of any kind. When you get to know me better, you will esteem me, for I swear to you I am estimable. I am extremely veracious, I love the truth, I hate change, I have suffered horribly for two years, I have been burned, I shall never go back, I am perfectly well: my heart, my mind, and my pride are equally content with you, what more could I desire, I am perfectly content. If you continue to be alarmed by the talk of gossips, do you know what I shall do? I shall lock myself up in my room and shall see no one but you, I must take extreme measures, and I love you more than my very self.

Letter 5:
Catherine to Potemkin (after 26 March 1774)

Sweetie, Grishenka, hello. I know, what will Praskovya Aleksandrovna say about me? She will say that I've lost my mind and my senses. And about you? Well, brother, you know for yourself what she'll say. I shan't guess, I'm not certain, I don't know, I'm afraid, I'm a coward. She will say, she will say, what will she say now? She will say: 'And he too loves her.' What else? Sweetheart, is it possible that these lines upset you? Have a good look, take note from where they spring. There is no reason to be angry. But no, it's time to stop giving you assurances. You must be most, most, most certain by now that I love you. And there you have the entire story, but some stories are not just stories. And still other stories – oh, but you've simply confused me. How bad it is for one with a mind to lose it! I want you to love me. I want to appear desirable to you. But I only show you madness and extreme weakness. Ugh, how bad it is to love so extraordinarily. It's an illness, you know. I'm ill, only I don't send for the chemist nor do I write long letters. If you want, I shall paraphrase this page for you in three words and cross out all the rest. Here it is: I love you.

Letter 6:

Catherine to Potemkin (c. March–April 1774)

Grishenka, hello. It seems to me this morning that not only do you love me and are affectionate, but that it's all with as much sincerity as I feel for you. And you must know, that those conclusions I draw in the morning become rules till such time as experience provides reasons for their refutation. But should you, contrary to any expectation and probability, use some sort of deception or cunning, then you ought to know that it's unforgivable for any intelligent person, as you are, to stick to such foolish methods when you yourself are the first and best method for controlling for life the heart and mind of a most sensitive person. Indeed, you know that this might well produce nothing but a certain kind of mistrust and anxiety not at all compatible with candour and sincerity, without which love can never be firmly established.

God be with you, brother, farewell. I am much smarter in the morning than at the setting of the sun. But be that as it may, my mind is upset. And should this continue, then I shall stop attending to my affairs, for I can't keep my mind on them, and I've been acting like a chicken with its head cut off. I truly shall try to use this week to my advantage, and may God grant me the reason and the good sense to seize the true path. For you know I've always been a *raisonneur de profession* ['philosophiser by trade'], although with the occasional delirium.

Letter 7:
Catherine to Potemkin (30 May 1774)
Tsarskoe Selo

General, do you love me? Me love general very much.

Letter 8:
Catherine to Potemkin (18 August 1774)
Lordikins, my angel, you should be the healthiest person in the world were your health to depend on my love for you.

Letter 9:
Catherine to Potemkin (c. March–December 1774)
Precious darling, although you don't need me in the least, still I need you very much. How's your health, and have I fallen out of favour or not? To you I proclaim God's as well as the empress's every blessing.

By 1776, the tone is changing. The insecurities, far from being assuaged, have taken deeper root. While it is apparent that Catherine and Potemkin feel deeply for each other, it is also becoming clear that they are unable to make one

another happy for much of the time. By the end of the year,
the affair was over, although the friendship remained for life.

Letter 10:

Catherine to Potemkin (c. February–March 1776)

Listening to you talk sometimes one might say that I am a
monster who has every possible shortcoming, particularly
that of being a beast. I am frightfully two-faced, and if
I'm grieved, if I cry, this is not the result of my sensibility
but something entirely different altogether, and this must
be ignored and I must be looked down upon. Such an
exceedingly tender way of behaving can only have a positive
effect on my mind. As mean and as horrible as this mind
is, however, it knows no other way of loving than to make
happy the one it loves. For this reason it's impossible for it
to be on bad terms with the one it loves even for a moment
without despairing, and it's even more impossible for it to be
continually occupied every moment of the day reproaching
the one it loves with this or that; on the contrary, my mind is
busy finding the virtues and merits in the one it loves. I love
to see in you all marvels. Pray tell, how would you behave if I
continuously reproached you for the shortcomings of all your
acquaintances, of all these whom you most respect or employ,
if I held you responsible for their blunders? Would you be
patient or impatient? If, seeing you impatient, I were to be
offended, were to get up, were to stomp away, slamming the

doors behind me, and after that were to be cold to you, were not to look at you, and were to act even colder than I in fact were; if I were to add threats to all this – would you conclude from this that I'd been putting on airs with you? Finally, if after this your head inflamed and your blood boiling, would it be most surprising if both of us had by then lost all common sense, if we couldn't understand each other or if we both spoke at the same time?

For Christ's sake, find the means to keep us from quarrelling ever again. Our quarrels always arise from nothing but irrelevant rubbish.

We quarrel about power, not about love. Now there's the truth for you. I know what you'll say, so don't bother saying it. For I shall indeed not answer you since, as concerns me, I, of course, do not intend to become impassioned. If you want to make me happy, speak to me of yourself. I shall never become angry.

Letter 11:
Potemkin to Catherine (c. February–March 1776; her annotations to his original note are included here, italicised in brackets)
Allow me, my precious dear, to say these final words (*I permit you*) that, I think, will end our row (*The sooner the better*). Don't be surprised that I am so uneasy about our love (*Be calm*). Beyond the innumerable gifts you've bestowed on

me (*One hand washes the other*), you've placed me in your heart (*Firmly and solidly*).

I want to be there alone (*You are and will be*), preferred to all former ones, since no one has so loved you as I (*I see and believe it*). And since I am the work of your hands, so I desire that you should secure my peace, that you should find joy (*I'm happy with all my soul*) in doing me good (*My foremost pleasure*), that you should devise everything for my comfort (*It'll come by itself*) and find therein repose from the great labours that occupy your lofty station.

Amen (*Let your thoughts be calm, so that your feelings can freely act; they are tender and will find the best way themselves. End of quarrel. Amen.*)

Letter 12:

Potemkin to Catherine (after 2 June 1776; Catherine's response is included, italicised, at the end)

Matushka [his pet-name for her, equating to 'Little Mother'], here is the result of your agreeable treatment of me over the past several days. I clearly see your inclination to get along with me. But you have let things go so far that it is becoming impossible for you to be kind to me. I came here to see you since without you life is tedious and unbearable. I noticed that you were incommoded by my arrival. I do not know whom or what you are trying to please; I only know that it is not necessary and to no purpose. It seems to me you have never before been so ill at ease.

Your Most Gracious Majesty, I shall go through fire
for you. But if it has finally been decided that I am to be
banished from you, then at least let it not be before the entire
public. I do not tarry to withdraw, although this is equal to
losing my life.

*(My friend, your imagination deceives you. I am glad to see you and
am not embarrassed by you. Rather I was vexed by an unrelated matter,
which I shall tell you about when an opportunity permits.)*

George IV, Maria Fitzherbert
and Caroline of Brunswick

George, the first child of King George III and Charlotte of Mecklenburg-Strelitz, became heir to the throne on his birth on 12 August 1762 at St James's Palace in London. Upon entering adulthood, he threw himself into a life of rakish excess, in the process becoming the epitome of late-eighteenth century dandyism. He caroused, womanised and gambled his way around London and kept the company of divisive figures that included the socialite Beau Brummell and the radical Whig politician, Charles James Fox. George's lifestyle was in stark contrast with that of his father, who had tended towards sober living, albeit regularly tempered by bouts of mental infirmity. The prince and his father regularly locked horns, all the while as the younger man built up a bank of scandal and debt.

While in his early twenties, George was introduced to Maria Fitzherbert and soon became obsessed with her. She met few of the criteria then required for a potential royal bride. Six years older than the prince, she was a twice-widowed commoner and, to top it all, a Roman Catholic – since 1701 it was legally prohibited to hold the throne if married to a Catholic. Nonetheless, at Maria's Mayfair home, towards the end of 1785, the couple went through a marriage ceremony of sorts. It could not have legal standing, since George was also required by law to have the consent of his father, but the pair seemingly treated it as the real thing. She considered herself his 'wife', despite the union lacking both legal and public acknowledgement.

All the while, George racked up more debt – he ran up a tab to various creditors equivalent to several million pounds in modern money. So, in 1787 he sought a grant from Parliament that would dig him out of his financial hole. There was a problem, though. Rumour of his marriage to Maria had spread and there was legitimate concern that, were it to become known to the public at large, there would be a scandal on a giant scale. George thus effectively denied the marriage in return for government financial support – a move that for a time threatened to end his ties to Fitzherbert altogether.

A year or so later, it seemed likely that George would ascend to the throne when his father was overtaken by a savage and prolonged bout of mental illness. However, the king recovered sufficiently to carry on in his position. As for the prince, the parliamentary cash injection helped for a while, but his excessive spending soon brought his old problems back. Moreover, George III, weary at his son's lack of self-discipline, stipulated that further help was dependent on him marrying a suitable bride. Princess Caroline of Brunswick was the well-connected woman hand-picked for him and finally, in 1795, Prince George agreed to the match. The wedding ceremony took place on 8 April that year in the Chapel Royal at St James's Palace. Yet even by the standard of arranged royal marriages, this was an ill-fitting one. It is said he was drunk at the ceremony itself, and did little to hide the fact that he did not find Caroline attractive. He also confided to friends that he doubted her virginal purity, without a hint of irony. Yet, somewhat remarkably, a daughter, Charlotte, was born in 1796 – almost exactly nine months after the nuptials – but her arrival effectively ended the parents' union. They parted within a few months and lived separately for the remainder of their lives.

As for Maria Fitzherbert, George's marriage to Caroline had served as a disavowal of their earlier 'marriage'. The prince spent several years distancing himself from her, frequently by brutally condemning her, but they remained in a relationship of sorts – albeit intermittent – until the end of his days. In addition, he had a string of lovers over the years from across the classes, but perhaps most notably Frances Villiers, Countess of Jersey. It is alleged he fathered several illegitimate children, too.

Caroline, freed from the day-to-day shackles of an unhappy marriage, also had other relationships. This might well have gone overlooked had not allegations emerged in 1805 (from a source with whom she was in dispute on other matters at the time) that a boy she had adopted three years earlier was in fact her own child. The following year, a commission including the prime minister was established in secret to look into the truth of the claims. Known as the 'Delicate Investigation', Caroline's private life was minutely dissected. In the end, it was shown beyond reasonable doubt that the boy was not her natural child, but by then her reputation had been destroyed.

In 1811, George III was so ill that he could no longer carry out his duties and so his dissolute son was given the powers to rule as Prince Regent. Caroline cut an increasingly lonely figure in England. When the approaching end of the Napoleonic Wars made a return to the European mainland plausible, she struck an agreement by which she effectively agreed to go into exile in return for a pension. Meanwhile, her daughter Princess Charlotte died in 1817 from complications following a stillbirth.

When George III died in 1820, the Prince Regent took to the throne in his own right. Little in his personal life or that of the country changed dramatically, though. Stylistically, it was a dynamic time – John Nash, a favourite architect of the new king, reconfigured the London landscape, while George's Eastern-influenced Royal Pavilion in Brighton remains a monument to the trends and excesses of the age.

Personally, George was drinking more than ever and was likely addicted to other substances too, so that the king cut a grossly obese figure upon the throne.

There was a perhaps appropriately dismal denouement to the marriage of George and Caroline. Although George investigated the possibility of divorce, he was advised against pursuing it so as to avert the risk of his assorted indiscretions coming under the public gaze. Although the couple had lived apart for almost a quarter of a century, the marriage was formally still intact. Caroline thus decided to return from the Continent for his coronation at Westminster Abbey on 19 July 1821, where she was intent on asserting her rights as the king's wife. He, though, wanted no more to do with her and instructed that she be barred entry from the abbey. Duly and humiliatingly, she was met at the church doors by bayonet-wielding guards. She fell ill later that day and died just a few weeks later, on 7 August, claiming that she had been poisoned.

The king reigned for a further ten years, a figure mocked and largely unloved by his subjects. By the late 1820s he was taking copious volumes of laudanum to get through his duties. He was eating and drinking more than ever, too. For example, in 1830 the Duke of Wellington reported a breakfast where George consumed 'a Pidgeon and Beef Steak Pye … Three parts of a bottle of Mozelle, a Glass of Dry Champagne, two Glasses of Port [and] a Glass of Brandy', all taken with a laudanum chaser. He died at Windsor Castle in the early hours of 26 June 1830, the result of various ailments including a burst blood vessel in the stomach, a large tumour and a weak heart. A letter from Maria Fitzherbert lay under his pillow.

The Letters

*The following series of notes is something of a curiosity. It appeared in anonymised form in a pamphlet that was distributed in London in 1785, under the title: 'Letters between an Illustrious Personage and a Lady of Honour at B******** [Brighton]'. Despite the anonymisation, it was clearly intended that the readership should understand these were love letters between Prince George and Maria Fitzherbert. Their true authorship is, though, a question of significant uncertainty. Nonetheless, the letters subsequently appeared in several volumes as genuine correspondence between the pair. So, while it may be that they are an example of epistolatory fiction, they offer the tantalising promise of a view on to the extraordinary affair of the prince and his 'other wife'. Note that Maria is referred to as Margaritta throughout.*

Letter 1:

Maria to George

> 'Princes, like women, find few real friends;
>
> All who approach them their own ends pursue,
>
> Lovers and ministers are seldom true.'

So spake a bard well used to courts and my sex. To you, my Prince, I ought, agreeable to the style of those who surround you, pay an implicit obedience, and meet you as you desired on my quitting the ballroom last night. Meet you! What, you, the Prince of Wales, whose character in the annals of gallantry is too well known for me to suppose that, after such a meeting, I should have any character at all? This may be too free — I am unused to address people of excessive rank — my manners are unaffected — I know not a sentiment that I would wish to disguise, and I should be happy to know only that behaviour from Your Royal Highness that must command silent respect from

> Your father's affectionate subject,
>
> Margaritta

Letter 2:

George to Maria

I find but too often cause to lament that rank in life that perhaps is envied me by all the world. Princes indeed have few real friends. Even your sex fly me, and does the amiable

Margaritta allow her better judgement to be biased by public calumny? It is beneath the heart that reigns in so lovely a bosom! I do not command, far from it, I only entreat a further knowledge of you, and where is the impropriety of permitting a meeting with a condescension that will make me most happy – not your prince, the son of your sovereign, but your admiring,

your adoring,

Wales

Letter 3:

Maria to George

Public calumny I am above; my own reasons and observation are the charms that forbid a private meeting. Already has the notice bestowed on me at the ball by Your Royal Highness brought on me the envy of my own sex and the impertinence of yours. I like not your associates, particularly that wild man, H., [presumably George Hanger] who stares me out of countenance. The difference of our rank in life forbids a further knowledge of me, and I entreat you to avoid me. I shall be tonight at the ball, not because I like it, but my not having appeared since the last is, I find, observed; and some of our visitors yesterday told me I was too much engaged by the prince's notice to bestow any on those beneath him. Come to the ball, dance with Lady B., and take the slightest notice of me. Why should you wish to take more? There are a hundred much prettier women! Mrs. O., for example – you think her pretty. She is indeed divine! And she has a husband, an officer of spirit, to shield her from the rude attacks of envy. You may enjoy her conversation, she yours, and malice dare not speak. But me, an unprotected, helpless orphan? It will be cruel to pursue the humble,

> Margaritta

Letter 4:

George to Maria

Cold – unkind – Margaritta!

Why am I forbid that attention that is your due – that all the world must pay you? Why am I doomed to pass an insipid evening with a woman of fashion only, when my heart and my better judgement would lead me to the most elegant, the most accomplished fair that Brighton has to boast. Mrs. O. is beauteous, but it is not mere beauty I admire, it is expression, 'a something than beauty dearer.' You know my opinion of Lady B.; her rank entitles her to my hand, nothing besides could induce me. I respect her Grace for the sake of the best of mothers, and therefore I comply with what politeness and etiquette requires; but why must I give up the enjoyment of your conversation? Be superior to common talk. Call not yourself unprotected – all the world must be your friends. I am concerned H. displeases you. I am certain he never designed it. This wild man has really some good points; that he admires you I wonder not, and perhaps he is not perfectly delicate in that admiration. Does S. [Richard Brinsley Sheridan, playwright and friend of the prince] likewise displease you, and little J. O. [John Willet Payne, known as 'Little Jacko'; another intimate of the prince, with a reputation as a scoundrel], that you say you do not like my associates? If they do, they shall not trouble you; I want no company when in yours! I felt your absence from the ball, and rejoice that you will grace it this evening. It is impossible to see you with indifference! In vain would you exact so hard a task from the tenderest of your friends,

The obliged,

Wales

Letter 5:

Maria to George

Surprised that I was not at the ball! Recollect your letter in the morning: it is impossible to see you with indifference. What then was I to expect? No one thing that I wished. You imagine, I doubt not, that my vanity would have been so well gratified that reason would have been silent. Had I suffered the woman wholly to prevail, this must have been the case; but a thousand combining circumstances have almost quelled the foibles of my sex, and vanity you must suppose dead in me when I withdraw thus from your notice. And yet I wish your friendship, am deeply interested in your fame, and desire most ardently that you may be as eminent in goodness as in rank. I cannot receive your visits; the family I am with would leave the place immediately on such an event.

... If you write again, be cautious how your letter is given me. I think it needless to desire you to destroy mine. They have no merit to entitle them to preservation; and as they are not directed or signed with my real name, I think they can never be made public. Yet I am not without fear. Such trash would be a treasure to the printer, and the very initials of your name would sell a book wonderfully.

Adieu.

Letter 6:

George to Maria

Do you indeed wish for my friendship! Ah! Margaritta, I know not how to believe you; while thus cold, thus insensible to all my desires. A meeting again refused; who are these very good people whom I have so much reason to dislike, they have no parental authority I understand; why then regard their narrow prejudices? May I entreat your history. Yet I almost dread to hear an account of a life in which I am already so much interested, and which may make me still more enamoured of the dear perverse historian. Politics I should never have mentioned to a lady, but as you seem to blame my conduct, I wish to exculpate myself in your opinion, but you must allow me to do it personally, for the subject is too long for a letter. On horseback you might permit me the pleasure of attending you, I have seen you riding with only a servant; let me join you without any; and I never ride but with one here, and he shall be forbid, because my livery would carry a mark that you would not like. Your servant would not know me, and report would have nothing to say about. I entreat you to allow me this, and appoint an early day. Your letters I keep as an invaluable treasure, and shall hardly be so careless of them as you expect. So young, so lovely and yet so coldly prudent. Ah, Margaritta, would that you partook of the warmth that burns in the heart of your faithful

Wales

Letter 7:

George to Maria

You reject all my wishes with a haughty disdain, which greatly mortifies me. I am open to correction; I avow my errors. I wish you to assume a character that you are most fit to shine in, and that may be of infinite service to me; but I wish, I entreat in vain! Unkind Margaritta. Even the words of an author I passionately admire [Shakespeare] is quoted against me. Thus you turn me from a book I might profit from; for when I attempt to read it, it reminds me of the cold, the severe fair one, whose friendship I have most wished to cultivate; who attributes to me all the faults of my predecessor Hal; and believe me incapable to finish the character. Am I to answer all the idle, the unjust things you hear to my disadvantage? Pardon my heat, I am disappointed! Hurt I acknowledge; but my heart feels now much more so at the sickly pale of the finest cheek that I beheld this morning! Had I not some merit when I met you on horseback not to join you? I debated it for half a moment; but the reserved air with which you returned my compliments determined me. I was repaid in the look you afterwards gave me; for I thought in that look you approved my discretion. Sickness only I hope has chilled that heart formed for more generous sensations. Your restoration to tender feelings. Judge for yourself, if I am not your attentive

Telemachus [a figure from Greek mythology]

Letter 8:

Maria to George

... when you talk of love, you offer an insult you are insensible of. Your friendship confers honour; but your love retains it for some worthy fair, born to the high honour of becoming your wife, and do not fret that fate has placed my lot in humble life. I am content with my station; content has charms that are not to be expressed. I know I am wrong in continuing this correspondence; it must, it ought to cease; write therefore no more to,

Margaritta

Letter 9:

George to Maria

You alarm me with the idea of your leaving Brighton; you pain me with your coldness. Ah, Margaritta, would it were possible to entreat your acceptance of the hand where the heart is all your own. Why is this forbid me? Cruel situation, forbid that highest pleasure that every subject enjoys. I cannot but fret! Tempers calm as yours may endure without complaining; you have suffered; you have learned to bear: but I, bred up with high hopes; young, warm, and sanguine, disappointment is a dagger that wounds most sorely! Do not then most amiable of women. Oh, do not add to my misfortunes your displeasure. Forgive a conduct I already see the impropriety of; allow for my unhappy situation ... deprive me not of your friendship, of your valued presence; your inestimable letters: but try to give comfort to that heart that is all your own ...

The next letter is an extract from a forty-two-page opus that George sent Maria in late 1785, shortly before their marriage ceremony (as quoted in Anita Leslie's 1960 work, Miss Fitzherbert: A Biography*).*

Letter 10:

George to Maria (3 November 1785)

I hardly know, my dearest and only beloved Maria, how I am to begin this letter to you. Such a train of extraordinary and wonderful events have happened lately, which at first created the greatest apprehensions and alarms in my bosom, and since have tended to the facilitating and entire arrangement of our plan, so that nothing now is wanting but the arrival of my adored wife in this country to make me the happiest of men, that I can hardly persuade myself that I have not been in a dream for these ten days past ...

I shall not add another syllable, but leave the decision of this affair to what you may think my merits are respecting you, to the sincerity of my attachment, and to my not having a wish nor a desire in life that does not centre in you, in short I trust the whole of your generosity. Come then, oh come, dearest of wives, best and most sacred of women, come and forever crown with bliss, him who will through life endeavour to convince you by his love and attention of his wishes to be the best of husbands and who will ever remain unto the latest moments of his existence unalterably yours ...

This excerpt from George's will, written in January 1796, shortly after Caroline had given birth to their daughter Charlotte, lays to rest any doubt as to the sincerity with which George and Maria at the time regarded their vows.

From George IV's will

By this, my last will and testament, I now bequeath, give, and settle at my death, all my worldly property of every description, denomination, and sort, personal and other, to Maria Fitzherbert, my wife, the wife of my heart and soul. Although by the laws of this country she could not avail herself publicly of that name, still such she is in the eyes of Heaven, was, is, and ever will be such in mine.

The notes above are in stark contrast with the letters between George and Caroline that follow, and which document a marriage not so much in decline as stillborn. The first short extract comes from a longer letter written by the prince in response to a missive Caroline had sent him concerning a number of issues. Not the least of these was her displeasure at having her husband's lover, Frances Villiers, in her household. He is unrepentant and berates Caroline before suggesting they accept their union is doomed. There then follow various negotiations as to how their domestic circumstances should be redefined.

Letter 1:
George to Caroline (21 April 1796)
We have unfortunately been obliged to acknowledge to each other that we cannot find happiness in our union. Circumstances of character and education ... render that impossible. It then only remains that we should make the situation as little uncomfortable to each other as its nature will allow ... Let me therefore beg you to make the best of a situation unfortunate for us both.

Letter 2:

George to Caroline (30 April 1796)

Windsor Castle

Madam

As Lord Cholmondeley informs me that you wish I would define, in writing, the terms upon which we are to live, I shall endeavour to explain myself upon that head with as much clearness, and with as much propriety as the nature of the subject will admit.

Our inclinations are not in our power, nor should either of us be held answerable to the other, because nature has not made us suitable to each other. Tranquillity and comfortable society are, however, in our power: let our intercourse, therefore, be restricted to those, and I will distinctly subscribe to the condition that you required, through Lord Cholmondeley, that even in the event of any accident happening to my daughter, which I trust Providence in its mercy will avert, I shall not infringe the terms of the restriction, by proposing a connection of a more particular nature. I shall now finally close this disagreeable correspondence, trusting that, as we have completely explained ourselves to each other, the rest of our lives will be passed in uninterrupted tranquillity.

I am, madam, with great truth, very sincerely yours,

George P.

Letter 3:

Caroline to George (6 May 1796)

Sir,

The avowal of your conversation with Lord Cholmondeley neither surprises nor offends me: it merely confirmed what you have tacitly insinuated for this twelve month. But, after this, it would be a want of delicacy, or rather an unworthy meanness in me, were I to complain of those conditions that you impose upon yourself.

I should have returned no answer to your letter, if it had not been conceived in terms to make it doubtful whether this arrangement proceeds from you or from me; and you are well aware that the credit belongs to you alone.

The letter that you announce to me as the last obliges me to communicate to the king, as to my sovereign and my father, both your avowal and my answer. You will find enclosed the copy of my letter to the king. I apprise you of it, that I may not incur the slightest reproach of duplicity from you. As I have at this moment no protector but His Majesty, I refer myself solely to him upon this subject; and if my conduct meets his approbation, I shall be in some degree at least consoled. I retain every sentiment of gratitude for the situation in which I find myself, as Princess of Wales, enabled by your means to indulge in the free exercise of a virtue dear to my heart – I mean charity.

It will be my duty, likewise, to act upon another motive – that of giving an example of patience and resignation under every trial. Do me the justice to believe that I shall never cease to pray for your happiness, and to be your much devoted

Caroline

Letter 4:

Caroline to George (14 January 1813)

Montague House [London]

Sir,

It is with great reluctance that I presume to obtrude myself upon Your Royal Highness, and to solicit your attention to matters that may, at first, appear rather of a personal than a public nature. If I could think them so – if they related merely to myself – I should abstain from a proceeding that might give uneasiness, or interrupt the more weighty occupations of Your Royal Highness's time. I should continue, in silence and retirement, to lead the life that has been prescribed to me, and console myself for the loss of that society and those domestic comforts to which I have so long been a stranger, by the reflection that it has been deemed proper I should be afflicted without any fault of my own – and that Your Royal Highness knows it.

But, sir, there are considerations of a higher nature than any regard to my own happiness, which render this address a duty both to myself and my daughter. May I venture to say – a duty also to my husband, and the people committed to his care? There is a point beyond which a guiltless woman cannot with safety carry her forbearance. If her honour is invaded, the defence of her reputation is no longer a matter of choice; and it signifies not whether the attack be made openly, manfully, and directly – or by secret insinuation, and by holding such conduct towards her, as countenances all the suspicions that malice can suggest. If these ought to be the feelings of every woman in England who is conscious that she deserves no reproach, Your Royal Highness has too sound a judgement, and too nice a sense of honour, not to perceive, how much more justly they belong to the mother of your daughter – the mother of her who is destined, I trust, at a very distant period, to reign over the British Empire.

It may be known to Your Royal Highness, that during the continuance of the restrictions upon your royal authority, I purposely refrained from making any representations that might then augment the painful difficulties of your exalted station. At the expiration of the restrictions I still was inclined to delay taking this step, in the hope that I might owe the redress I sought to your gracious and unsolicited condescension. I have waited in the fond indulgence of this expectation, until, to my inexpressible mortification, I find that my unwillingness to complain has only produced fresh grounds of complaint; and I am at length compelled, either to abandon all regard to the two dearest objects that I possess on Earth – mine own honour, and my beloved child – or to throw myself at the feet of Your Royal Highness, the natural protector of both.

I presume, sir, to represent to Your Royal Highness, that the separation, which every succeeding month is making wider, of the mother and the daughter, is equally injurious to my character, and to her education. I say nothing of the deep wounds that so cruel an arrangement inflict upon my feelings, although I would feign hope that few persons will be found of a disposition to think lightly of these. To see myself cut off from one of the very few domestic enjoyments left to me – certainly the only one upon which I set any value, the society of my child, involves me in such misery, as I well know Your Royal Highness could never inflict upon me, if you were aware of its bitterness. Our intercourse has been gradually diminished. A single interview weekly seemed sufficiently hard allowance for a mother's affections. That however, was reduced to our meeting once a fortnight; and I now learn, that even this most rigorous interdiction is to be still more rigidly enforced.

... The powers with which the constitution of these realms vest Your Royal Highness in the regulation of the royal family, I know, because I am so advised, are ample and unquestionable. My appeal, sir, is made to your excellent sense and liberality of mind in the exercise of those powers: and I willingly hope, that your own parental feelings will lead you to excuse the anxiety of mine, by impelling me to represent the unhappy consequences that the present system must entail upon our beloved child.

... Those who have advised you, sir, to delay so long the period of my daughter's commencing her intercourse with the world, and for that purpose to make Windsor her residence, appear not to have regarded the interruptions to her education that this arrangement occasions ... To the same unfortunate counsels I ascribe a circumstance in every way so distressing, both to my parental and religious feelings, that my daughter has never yet enjoyed the benefit of confirmation, although above a year older than the age at which all the other branches of the royal family have partaken of that solemnity. May I earnestly conjure you, sir, to hear my entreaties upon this serious matter, even if you should listen to other advisers on things of less near concernment to the welfare of your child?

The pain with which I have at length formed the resolution of addressing myself to Your Royal Highness is such as I should in vain attempt to express. If I could adequately describe it, you might be enabled, sir, to estimate the strength of the motives that have made me submit to it: they are the most powerful feelings of affection, and the deepest impressions of duty towards Your Royal Highness, my beloved child, and the country that I devoutly hope she may be preserved to govern and to show, by a new example, the liberal affection of a free and generous people to a virtuous and constitutional monarch.

I am, sir, with profound respect, and an attachment that nothing can alter, Your Royal Highness's most devoted and most affectionate consort, cousin, and subject,

(Signed) Caroline Louisa

Letter 5:

Caroline to George (26 May 1814)

Connaught House [London]

Sir,

I am once more reluctantly compelled to address Your Royal Highness, and to enclose for your inspection, copies of a note, which I have had the honour to receive from the queen, and of the answer that I have thought it my duty to return to Her Majesty. It would be in vain for me to enquire into the reasons of the alarming declaration made by Your Royal Highness, that you have taken the fixed and unalterable determination never to meet me, upon any occasion, in either public or private. Of these Your Royal Highness is pleased to state yourself to be the only judge ... I owe it to myself, to my daughter, and to the nation, to which I am deeply indebted for the vindication of my honour, to remind Your Royal

Highness of what you know; that after open persecution and mysterious inquiries, upon undefined charges, the malice of my enemies fell entirely upon themselves; and that I was restored by the king, with the advice of his ministers, to the full enjoyment of my rank in his court, upon my complete acquittal. Since His Majesty's lamented illness, I have demanded, in the face of Parliament and the country, to be proved guilty, or to be treated as innocent. I have been declared innocent – I will not submit to be treated as guilty.

Sir, Your Royal Highness may possibly refuse to read this letter; but the world must know that I have written it; and they will see my real motives for foregoing, in this instance, the rights of my rank. Occasions, however, may arise (one, I trust is far distant) when I must appear in public, and Your Royal Highness must be present also. Can Your Royal Highness have contemplated the full extent of your declaration? Has Your Royal Highness forgotten the approaching marriage of our daughter, and the possibility of our coronation? I waive my rights in a case where I am not absolutely bound to assert them, in order to relieve the queen, as far as I can, from the painful situation in which she is placed by Your Royal Highness; not from any consciousness of blame, not from any doubt of the existence of these rights, or of my own worthiness to enjoy them. Sir, the time you have selected for this proceeding is calculated to make it peculiarly galling. Many illustrious strangers

are already arrived in England; among others, as I am
informed, the illustrious heir of the house of Orange, who
has announced himself to me as my future son-in-law. From
their society I am unjustly excluded. Others are expected,
of rank equal to your own, to rejoice with Your Royal
Highness in the peace of Europe. My daughter will, for the
first time, appear in the splendour and publicity becoming
the approaching nuptials of the presumptive heiress of
this empire. This season Your Royal Highness has chosen
for treating me with fresh and unprovoked dignity; and of
all His Majesty's subjects, I alone am prevented by Your
Royal Highness from appearing in my place, to partake of
the general joy; and am deprived of the indulgence in those
feelings of pride and affection, permitted to every mother
but me. I am, sir, Your Royal Highness's faithful wife,

Caroline P.

Letter 6:

Caroline to George (7 August 1820)

Brandenburgh House [London]

Sir,

After the unparalleled and unprovoked persecution
that, during a series of years, has been carried on against
me, under the name and authority of Your Majesty – and
which persecution, instead of being modified by time,
time has rendered only more and more malignant and

unrelenting – it is not without a great sacrifice of private feeling that I now, even in the way of remonstrance, bring myself to address this letter to Your Majesty. But bearing in mind that 'Royalty rests on the basis of Public Good'; that to this paramount consideration all others ought to submit; and aware of the consequences that may result from the present unconstitutional, illegal, and hitherto unheard-of proceedings – with a mind thus impressed, I cannot refrain from laying my grievous wrongs once more before Your Majesty, in the hope that the justice that Your Majesty may, by evil-minded counsellors, be still disposed to refuse to the claims of a dutiful, faithful and injured wife, you may be induced to yield to considerations connected with the honour and dignity of your crown, the stability of your throne, the tranquillity of your dominions, the happiness and safety of your just and loyal people, whose generous hearts revolt at oppression and cruelty, and especially when perpetrated by a perversion and a mockery of the laws.

A sense of what is due to my character and sex forbids me to refer minutely to the real causes of our domestic separation, or to the numerous unmerited insults offered me previously to that period; but, leaving to Your Majesty to reconcile with the marriage vow the act of driving, by such measures, a wife from beneath your roof, with an infant in her arms, Your Majesty will permit me to remind you, that that act was entirely your own; that the separation, so far from being sought for by me, was a sentence pronounced upon me, without any cause assigned, other than inclinations, which as Your Majesty was pleased to allege, were not under your control.

Not to have felt, with regard to myself, chagrin at this decision of Your Majesty's, would have argued great insensibility to the obligations of decorum; not to have dropped a tear in the face of that beloved child, whose future sorrows were then but too easy to foresee, would have marked me as unworthy of the name of mother; but, to have submitted to it without repining, would have indicated a consequence of demerit, or a want of those feelings, that belong to affronted and insulted female honour.

... In withdrawing from the embraces of my parents, in giving my hand to the son of George III and the heir apparent to the British throne, nothing less than a voice from Heaven would have made me fear injustice or wrong of any kind. What, then, was my astonishment at finding that treasons against me had been carried on and matured, perjuries against me had been methodised and embodied, a secret tribunal had been held, a trial of my actions had taken place, and a decision had been made upon those actions, without my having been informed of the nature of the charge, or of the names of the witnesses, and what words can express the feelings excited by the fact, that this proceeding was founded on a request made, and on evidence furnished, by order of the father of my child, and my natural as well as legal guardian and protector?

... I have now frankly laid before Your Majesty a statement of my wrongs, and a declaration of my views and intentions. You have cast upon me every slur to which the female character is liable. Instead of loving, honouring, and cherishing me, agreeably to your solemn vow, you have pursued me with hatred and scorn, and with all the means of destruction you wrested from me my child, and with her my only comfort and consolation. You sent me sorrowing through the world, and even in my sorrows, pursued me with unrelenting persecution. Having left me nothing but my innocence, you would now, by a mockery of justice, deprive me even of the reputation of possessing that.

The poisoned bowl and the dagger are means more manly than perjured witnesses and partial tribunals; and they are less cruel, insomuch as life is less valuable than honour. If my life would have satisfied Your Majesty, you should have had it, on the sole condition of giving me a place in the same tomb with my child: but, since you would send me dishonoured to the grave, I will resist the attempt with all the means that it shall please God to give me.

Caroline R.

Napoleon Bonaparte, Joséphine,
Maria Walewska and Marie Louise

Napoleon was born Napoleone di Buonaparte on 15 August 1769 in Ajaccio, on the island of Corsica, to Carlo Buonaparte and his wife, Letizia. Corsica, which had enjoyed several years as an independent republic, was traditionally under the jurisdiction of the Republic of Genoa, but came under French control in the year of Napoleon's birth.

Napoleon's early upbringing reflected his family's long-standing Italian heritage, while politically his parents supported the cause of Corsican independence. Napoleon thus did not begin to learn the French language until he was ten or so years old. Then, in 1784, aged fifteen, he entered the École Militaire in Paris and was duly commissioned into the French army. His sympathies remained with the cause of Corsican independence but his world would be turned upside-down by the onset of the French Revolution in 1789. Having allied himself with the principles of the revolutionaries, in 1795 he was key to suppressing a royalist uprising against the National Convention – the assembly charged with drawing up designs for the new Republic of France following the guillotining of Louis XVI.

Napoleon's mastery of military strategy was already apparent to his military superiors but his exploits in downing this rebellion won him fame among the wider public too. With the Directory soon succeeding the National Convention as France's government, Napoleon was rewarded for his exploits with the titles of Commander of the Interior and of the Italian Army. Having become engaged to a wealthy merchant's daughter, Désirée Clary, in 1795, he broke off the attachment (she later became queen consort of Sweden and Norway) when he fell in love with Joséphine de Beauharnais, a former mistress of leading revolutionary figure Paul Barras. She was some six years older than Napoleon and had already been married. Her first husband, Alexandre de Beauharnais, was executed in 1794, just days prior to the fall of Maximilien Robespierre and the end of the Reign of Terror – an event that saw Joséphine freed from her own incarceration. Napoleon fell deeply in love with her, they were married in March 1796 and he formally adopted her children.

But within days of the union, he was bound for Italy to lead his army, where his exploits in subduing the Italian peninsula made him a hero back home. As his military reputation rose, spurred on by a string of notable victories across Europe and beyond, so did his political capital. In 1799, he spearheaded a coup against the increasingly unpopular

Directory and was installed as First Consul of the Republic. As the dominant figure in the nation's politics, five years later he was crowned emperor with Joséphine at his side. For a decade more he remained arguably the most important figure in European life as he fought a seemingly endless round of battles against his many enemies – among them, Britain, Prussia, Russia, Sweden, Austria, Spain and Portugal.

Domestically, Napoleon and Joséphine both had affairs early in the marriage – she notably with a military man called Hippolyte Charles, and he with Pauline Bellisle Fourès (whom he called 'Cleopatra'), the wife of one of his junior officers. Nonetheless, these were largely distractions to the bigger picture of their love story, which endured even after their divorce in 1810. Had she borne him a son and heir, it is unlikely that they would have split, but Napoleon became desperate to secure his succession and so the sacrifice was made. Within a few weeks of their parting, he married (by proxy) Archduchess Marie Louise of Austria.

By then, Napoleon already had at least one illegitimate child, a son born in 1806 to his mistress Eléonore Denuelle de La Plaigne. The boy served as evidence that Napoleon was not infertile – a fact that likely hastened the end of his marriage to Joséphine. But there were several other lovers along the way, perhaps most significantly Maria Walewska, who almost certainly had a son by him (although her husband claimed him as his own). Napoleon and the Polish Walewska started their relationship around 1806 and there is reason to believe that she was initially used as a political pawn to win Napoleon's support for Polish independence against the various forces of Prussia, Russia and the Habsburgs. Regardless, she dutifully spent the next few years following him around Europe until his planned nuptials to Marie Louise compelled him to end the affair.

Marie Louise was a great niece of Marie Antoinette, of all people, and less than half her husband's age. She was not much taken with the idea of the partnership to begin with. Napoleon had been on the side of the revolutionaries who killed her great-aunt and had spent years fighting her country. But as time passed, her heart warmed to him. She would write to her father: 'He loves me very much. I respond to his love sincerely. There is something very fetching and very eager about him that is impossible to resist.' Then, in 1811, she gave him what he most desired, a son.

But despite promising omens, the stars were not aligned for a long and successful partnership. By 1814, Napoleon was battling the allied forces of Austria, Great Britain, Portugal, Prussia, Russia and Sweden. At last his military good fortune ran out as the allies invaded France and marched on Paris. The emperor was forced to abdicate and sent into exile on the island of Elba, off the Italian Tuscan coast. While there, news reached him of the death of Joséphine, prompting him to lock himself away and weep inconsolably for two days. He managed to escape his captivity a year later and led a counter-invasion that initially succeeded in retaking France, prompting the fabled 'hundred days' in which Napoleon again ruled, before the restoration of Louis XVIII as king. In the meantime, Marie Louise had fallen for the Austrian Count Adam Albert von Neipperg and passed a request to her husband that he should agree to an amicable parting of the ways, although she did not demand a formal divorce. He had not seen his wife or their child since his exile on Elba.

Napoleon suffered his last military defeat – against a British-led coalition – at the Battle of Waterloo in June that year (1815). He was again sent into exile, this time to the much more remote British possession of St Helena in the South Atlantic. He died there on 5 May 1821, having suffered a period of ill health exacerbated by his poor living conditions. Marie Louise married Neipperg three months later and, after being widowed once more, re-married in 1833. She died of pleurisy in 1847.

At the end of his life, Napoleon gave a clear indication of where his heart really lay. His last words were reportedly: '*France, l'armée, tête d'armée, Joséphine*' ('France, the army, head of the army, Joséphine').

The Letters

Napoleon was a brilliant military tactician and remarkable political force, but he was more than that, too. He became a cipher of a time, the personification of the spirit of the age. One can get a sense of his extraordinary character from these missives, which are divided into three sets. The first are to Joséphine and the heat and passion of his love for her burns through them. (It is worth noting, too, that Josephine seems not to have been quite such an ardent correspondent.) The second set, to Maria Walewska, are similarly heartfelt. We know Joséphine was his great love, but these notes to Maria, written against the backdrop of military and political endeavours that were reconfiguring Europe, reveal a man whose yearning for personal connection sat alongside his efforts to mould the international landscape. Finally, the letters to Marie Louise provide a glimpse of the great leader as the empire he had built began to collapse and he grimly faced, in the most literal sense, his Waterloo.

Letter 1:
Napoleon to Joséphine (c. 23 February 1796, a couple of weeks before their wedding)

7 o'clock in the morning

I awake with my thoughts full of you. Your portrait and the remembrance of the delirious evening of yesterday have not allowed rest to my senses. Sweet and incomparable Joséphine, what a strange influence you have on my heart. Are you cross? Do I see you sad? Are you uneasy? My soul is broken with grief, and there is no more rest for your beloved

... But is there more for me when, yielding ourselves up to the deep feeling that overcomes me, I pour out upon your lips, upon your heart, a flame that consumes me? Ah, it was last night that I thoroughly realised that your portrait was not you. You are going away at noon. I shall see you in three hours. Meanwhile, my sweet love, accept a thousand kisses, but do not give me any, for they burn up my blood,

    N. B.

Letter 2:

Napoleon to Joséphine (4 April 1796, when Napoleon was away with his army)

Port Maurice [Liguria, Italy]

I have received all your letters, but none has made such an impression on me as your last. How can you think, my adorable beloved, of writing to me in such terms? Do you imagine, then, that my position is not already sufficiently painful without further increasing my regrets and subverting my reason. What a style! What feelings do you portray – they are of fire, which burns my poor heart – my only Joséphine. Far from you there is no joy – away from you the world is a wilderness, where I remain alone without enjoying the sweetness of unburdening myself. You have robbed me of more than my soul – you are the only thought of my life. If I am tired of the worries of my profession, if I am fearful of its issue, if men disgust me, if I am ready to curse life, if I put my hand on my heart your portrait there beats. I look at it and love is for me absolute happiness, and all is smiling save for the time when I find myself parted from my beloved.

By what art have you become able to captivate all my faculties, to concentrate in yourself my moral existence? It is a magic, my sweet love, that will end only with me. To live for Joséphine, that is the history of my life. I am trying to reach you, I am dying to be near you. Fool that I am, I do not realise that I am far away from you, that lands and countries separate us. What a time it will be before you read these lines, these feeble expressions of a troubled soul wherein you reign. Ah, my adorable wife, I know not what fate awaits me, but if it keeps me much longer away from you, I shall not be able to bear it: my courage will not hold out so long. Time was when I prided myself on my courage, and sometimes when considering the evil that men might be able to do me, the fate that might have in store for me, I fixed my eyes steadfastly on the most unheard-of misfortunes without frowning, without being surprised; but today the idea that my Joséphine might be unwell, the idea that she might be ill, and, above all, the cruel, the fatal thought that she might love me less, withers my soul, stops my blood, makes me sad, cast down, and leaves me not even the courage of fury and despair. I often used to say to myself that men could have no power over him who dies without regrets. But today to die without being loved by you, to die without that certainty is the torment of hell, is the lifelike and striking image of absolute annihilation. I feel as if I were being stifled. My only companion, you whom fate has decreed to make with me the painful journey of life, the day when I shall no longer possess your heart will be that when parched Nature will be to me without warmth and without vegetation. I stop, my sweet beloved. My soul is sad, my body is tired, my mind is dazed, men worry me. I ought indeed to detest them: they separate me from my darling.

I am at Port Maurice, near Orneille. Tomorrow I am at Albenga. The two armies are moving. We are endeavouring to deceive each other. Victory to the most skilful! ... Do not be uneasy. Love me as your eyes – but that is not enough: as yourself, more than yourself; as your thoughts, your mind, your sight, your all. Sweet beloved, forgive me. I am worn out. Nature is weak for him who feels keenly, for him whom you love!

N. B.

... Good-bye, good-bye. I lie down ... I pray you let me sleep. Many times I hold you in my arms – happy thought – but, but it is not you.

Letter 3:

Napoleon to Joséphine (6 April 1796)

Albenga [Liguria, Italy]

It is one hour after midnight. They have just brought me a
letter. It is a sad one. My mind is distressed, it is the death of
Chauvet. He was commissaire ordinateur en chef of the army.
You have seen him sometimes at Barras' house. My darling,
I feel the need of being consoled. That is why I am writing
to you, to you alone, the thought of whom can so much
influence the moral condition of my ideas, to whom I must
pour out my troubles. What is the future? What is the past?
What are we ourselves? What magic fluid is it that surrounds
and hides the things that we must needs know most of all?
We are born, we live, we die in the midst of marvels. Is it
surprising that priests, astrologers, charlatans have profited
by this inclination, by this strange circumstance to exploit
our ideas and to guide them according to their passions?

Chauvet is dead. He was devoted to me. He has rendered
material service to the fatherland. His last words were that
he was starting off to join me. But yes, I see his ghost. It
wanders everywhere: it whistles in the air: his soul is in the
clouds: it will be propitious to my destiny. But fool that I am
I shed tears over our friendship and who shall tell me that I
have not already to bewail something irreparable? Soul of my
life, write to me by every courier. I should not know how to
live otherwise.

I am very busy here. Beaulieu [Johann Peter Beaulieu, enemy commander] is moving his army again. We are in sight. I am a little tired: I am every day on horseback. Good-bye, good-bye, good-bye. I am going to dream of you. Sleep consoles me: it places you by my side: I press you on my arms ... but on waking, alas! I find myself three hundred leagues away from you ...

N. B.

Letter 4:

Napoleon to Joséphine (8 April 1796)

I have received a letter in which you break off, to go, as you say to the country and after that you pretend to be jealous of me who is here, overwhelmed with business and fatigue. Ah, my darling, it is true that I am wrong. In the springtime the country is beautiful and then the lover of nineteen years old would doubtless find the means of snatching a moment more to write to him who is three hundred leagues from you, who lives, enjoys and exists only by remembrance of you, who reads your letters as one devours, after a six-hour hunt, his favourite dishes. I am not satisfied with your last letter: it is cold as friendship. I have not found therein that fire that lights up your looks, the fire that I believe I have seen there many a time. But how great is my infatuation. I found your previous letters weighed too heavily on my mind. The revolution that they there produced destroyed my repose and enslaved my senses.

I desired colder letters but they gave me the chill of death. The fear of not being loved by Joséphine, the idea of finding her inconstant, of ... but I am forging troubles. There are so many real ones, must one manufacture any more!!! You cannot have inspired me with a boundless love without sharing thereof, and with your soul, your thought, and your reason, one cannot requite complete surrender and devotion with the death blow.

... You say nothing about your wretched indigestion. I hate it. Good-bye till tomorrow *mio dolce amor*. A remembrance of my best of wives and a victory over destiny – these are my wishes. A solitary remembrance entirely worthy of he, who thinks of you every moment.

My brother is here. He has heard with delight of my marriage. He is most anxious to meet you. I am trying to get him to come to Paris. His wife has just been confined. She has presented him with a girl. He is sending you as a present a box of Genoese bonbons. You will receive some oranges, some perfumes and some orange-flower water, which I am sending you.

Letter 5:

Napoleon to Joséphine (25 April 1796)

Headquarters, Carru [Piedmont, Italy]

To my sweet beloved,

... I have received your letter of the 6th and 11th. You have been a good many days without writing me. What are you doing? Yes my dear, dear love, I am not jealous but sometimes uneasy. Come soon, I warn you if you delay you will find me ill. Fatigue and your absence are too much to have at once.

Your letters are my daily delight, and my happy days are not frequent. Junot [Jean-Andoche Junot, a French general] is bringing to Paris twenty-two flags. You must return with him. Do you understand? If that is not disagreeable to you. Should he not come, misfortune without remedy; grief without consolation; endless sufferings if I should have the misfortune to see him come alone. My adorable beloved, he will see you, he will breathe on your temples: maybe you will allow him the rare and priceless favour of kissing your cheek, and I – I shall be alone and very, very far away. But you will come, won't you? You are going to be here by my side, on my heart, in my arms, on my mouth. Take wings, come, come, but travel gently. The journey is long and very tiring. If you were to be overturned or to be taken ill, if the fatigue – go gently my adorable beloved but be often ... with me in thought ...

N. B.

I do not know if you need any money, for you never speak to me of business. If you do, ask my brother for some: he has 200 louis of mine.

N. B.

Letter 6:

Napoleon to Joséphine (16 June 1796)

Tortona [Piedmonte, Italy]

To Joséphine,

My life is a perpetual nightmare. A presentiment of ill
hinders me from breathing. I no longer live. I have lost more
than life, more than happiness, more than rest. I am almost
without hope. I am despatching a courier to you. He will
stay only four hours in Paris and then will bring me your
answer. Write me ten pages. That alone can console me a
little ... You are ill, you love me, I have made you unhappy.
You are in a delicate condition and I see you not. That
thought overwhelms me. I have done so many wrongs against
you that I know not how to atone for them. I accuse you of
remaining in Paris and you were there ill. Forgive me, my
darling. The love that you have inspired in me has taken away
my reason. I shall never recover it again. There is no cure
for that complaint. My presentiments are so ominous that
I would content myself with seeing you, with pressing you
for a couple of hours against my heart and then dying with
you. Who is taking care of you? I presume you have sent for
Hortense [Joséphine's daughter from her first marriage]. I
love that dear child a thousand times more since I think that
she can console you a little. As for me there is no consolation,
no repose, no hope until I have received the courier whom I
am sending to you, and until by a long letter you explain to

me what is the nature of your illness and how far it is serious. If it is dangerous, I warn you I set off immediately for Paris. My arrival will be a match for your illness. I have always been lucky. Never has my destiny resisted my will, and today I am struck on the one spot where I can feel anything. Joséphine, how can you remain so long without writing to me? Your last laconic letter is dated 23rd May. It is a painful one for me. However, I always have it in my pocket. Your portrait and your letters are ever before my eyes.

I am nothing without you. I scarcely imagine how I have existed without knowing you. Ah, Joséphine if you had known my heart would you have waited from 19th May to 5th June before starting? Would you have listened to false friends who wished, perhaps, to keep you away from me? I openly admit I hate everyone who is near you. I expected you to have set out on 25th May and to have arrived at Milan on 4th June.

Joséphine, if you love me, if you believe that everything depends on your keeping in good health, take care of yourself. I dare not tell you not to undertake a journey of such length and in the hot weather. At least if you are well enough to make the journey come by short stages. Write to me at every sleeping place and send me your letters ahead.

All my thoughts are concentrated in your boudoir, in your bed, on your heart. Your illness – that is what occupies my mind night and day. Without appetite, without sleep, without care for my friendships, for glory, for fatherland, you, you and the rest of the world exist no more for me than if it were annihilated. I prize honour since you prize it. I prize victory since that gives you pleasure, without which I should have left all to throw myself at your feet.

Sometimes I say to myself that I am needlessly alarmed, that already she is better, that she is setting out, she is perhaps already at Lyons. A foolish fancy! You are in your bed suffering, more beautiful, more interesting, more adorable. You are pale and your eyes are more languishing but when will you be well? If one of us two must be ill ought it not to be I? Stronger and braver I should have been able to bear illness more easily. Destiny is cruel: it attacks me through you.

What comforts me sometimes is to think that it is in the power of fate to make you ill, but that no one can compel me to survive you.

In your letter, my darling, be careful to tell me that you are convinced that I love you beyond all imagining, that you are persuaded that every moment of my life is consecrated to you, that never an hour passes without my thinking of you, that never has the thought of thinking of another woman entered my head, that to my eyes they are lacking in grace, beauty and wit, that you, you only, such as I see you, such as you are, could please me and absorb all the faculties of my mind; that you have influenced it all over, that my heart has no recesses which you do not see, no thoughts which are not subject to you; that my strength, my prowess, my spirit are all yours, that my soul is in your body, and that the day when you shall change or when you shall cease to live, will be my death-day; that nature, the earth are beautiful to my eyes only because you dwell therein. If you do not believe all that, if your mind is not convinced, penetrated by it, you distress me, you love me not. There is a magnetic fluid between people who love one another. You know quite well that I could not bear to let you have a lover, still less to offer you one. To tear out his heart and to see him would be the same thing for me. And then if I should dare to lay my hands on your sacred person – no, I should never dare to do so, but I would quit a life wherein that which is most virtuous should have deceived me.

But I am certain and proud of your love. Misfortunes are the trials that expose to both of us the full force of our passion. A child, as bewitching as its mother, will soon see daylight and will pass many years in your arms. Unhappy me! I would content myself with one day. A thousand kisses on your eyes, on your lips, on your tongue, on your heart. Most enchanting of women, what is your power over me? I am very ill of your malady. I have, besides, a burning fever. Do not keep the courier more than six hours and let him return immediately to bring me the longed-for letter of queen.

Do you remember the dream in which I was your shoes, your dress, and I made you enter deep into my heart. Why did not Nature arrange matters thus? There are many things that want doing.

N. B.

Letter 7:
Napoleon to Joséphine (27 June 1796)
Pistoia, Tuscany

To Joséphine,

For a month I have only received from my darling two letters of three lines each. Is she so busy? She does not then need to write to her beloved, much less to think of him. To live without thinking of Joséphine, this would be to your husband to be dead and not to exist. Your image adorns my thoughts and enlivens the black and sombre picture of melancholy and grief. A day will come perhaps when I shall see you, for I do not doubt that you are still in Paris, and truly on that day I will show you my pockets full of letters that I have not sent to you, because they were too stupid – yes, that's the word. Good heavens! Tell me, you who know so well how to make others love without being in love yourself, do you know how to cure me of love??? I will pay a good price for that remedy. You ought to have started on 25th May. Good-natured as I was, I waited till 2nd June, as if a pretty woman could give up her habits,

her friends ... You love everything more than your husband,
for him you have only a little esteem, and a portion of
that kindness with which your heart abounds. Every day I
reckon up your wrongdoings, your faults. I beat myself so
as not to love you any longer. Bah! Do I not love you still
more? In short, my dearest of little mothers, I am going to
tell you my secret. Laugh at me, remain in Paris, have your
lovers, let all the world know it, never write to me. Ah well
I shall love you for it ten times more. And it is not folly,
delirious fever!! And I shall never be cured of it. Oh, if by
heaven I could get better! But don't go and tell me you
are ill, don't try and justify yourself. Good heavens you are
forgiven. I love you to distraction, and never will my poor
heart cease to give you all for love. If you did not love me,
my lot would be indeed wretched. You have not written to
me: you were ill, you have not come ... Farewell, my well-
beloved, a kiss on your mouth, another on your heart, and
another on your little child.

We have made peace with Rome, which gives us money.
Tomorrow we shall be at Leghorn and as soon as possible in
your arms, at your feet, on your bosom.

*From these stormy, jealous sentiments to some lusty missives
to Marie Walewska.*

Letter 1:

Napoleon to Marie (January 1807)

Warsaw

I saw no one but you, I admired no one but you, I want no one but you. Answer me at once, and assuage the impatient passion of N.

Letter 2:

Napoleon to Marie (January 1807)

Warsaw

Didn't you like me, Madame? I had reason to hope you might ... Or perhaps I was wrong. Whilst my ardour is increasing, yours is slackening its pace. You are mining my repose! Ah, grant a few moments' pleasure and happiness to a poor heart that is only waiting to adore you. Is it so difficult to let me have an answer? You owe me two.

    N.

Letter 3:

Napoleon to Marie (January 1807)

Warsaw

There are times – I am passing through one now – when hope is as heavy as despair. What can satisfy the needs of a smitten heart, which longs to throw itself at your feet, but is held back by the weight of serious considerations, paralysing its keenest desires?

Oh, if only you would! ... No one but you can remove the obstacles that keep us apart ... Ah, come! come! You shall have all you ask. Your country will be dearer to me, once you have had pity on my poor heart.

N.

Letter 4:

Napoleon to Marie (January 1807)

Warsaw

Marie, my sweet Marie, my first thought is of you, my first desire is to see you again. You will come again, won't you? You promised you would.

If you don't, the eagle will fly to you! I shall see you at dinner – our friend tells me so. I want you to accept this bouquet: I want it to be a secret link, setting up a private understanding between us in the midst of the surrounding crowd. We shall be able to share our thoughts, though all the world is looking on. When my hand presses my heart, you will know that I am thinking of no one but you; and when you press your bouquet, I shall have your answer back!

Love me, my pretty one, and hold your bouquet tight!

N.

And, finally, to Marie Louise, the wife Napoleon had felt compelled to take. The final two letters date from shortly after Napoleon had been deposed as emperor, but before he had gone into exile.

Letter 1:

Napoleon to Marie Louise (1 November 1813)

Frankfurt [Germany]

Madame and beloved Wife,

I send you twenty flags taken by my armies at the battles of Wachau, Leipzig and Hanover: it is an homage that I delight in offering to you. I desire that you should see by this a mark of my great satisfaction with your conduct during the regency that I entrusted to you.

Napoleon

Letter 2:

Napoleon to Marie Louise (c. 19 April 1814)

Fontainebleau [France]

8 o'clock at night

My darling Louise,

I have received your letter; I see thereby all your sufferings, which increase mine. I see with delight that Corvisart [Jean-Nicolas Corvisart, Napoleon's physician] gives you encouragement. I am ever so much obliged to him; he justifies by that noble conduct all the good opinion that I have had of him, tell him this from me. Let him send me a brief bulletin, frequently, as to your condition. Try and go as soon as possible to the waters of Aix, which they tell me Corvisart has advised you to take. Get well soon, take care of your health for ... your son, who needs all your care.

I am going to start for the island of Elba, whence I will write you. I shall do everything also for your reception.

Write to me often, address your letters to the Viceroy and to your uncle if, as they say, he is made Grand Duke of Tuscany.

Farewell, my beloved Louise Marie.

Letter 3:

Napoleon to Marie Louise (20 April 1814)

Fontainebleau

9 o'clock in the morning

My darling,

I am setting out to sleep tonight at Briare. I shall start tomorrow morning so as not to stop anywhere till I reach Saint Tropez. Beausset [a trusted official], who will bring you this letter, will give you my news and will tell you that I am quite well and that I hope that your health will be maintained and that you will be able to come and join me. Montesquiou [Napoleon's chamberlain], who started at two o'clock in the morning, should have arrived. I have not got your news of yesterday, but am hoping that the prefect of the palace will join me this evening and will give it me. Farewell, my beloved Louise. You can always rely on the courage, the calmness, and the affection of your husband,

Napoleon.

A kiss to the little king [their son Napoleon II, who had enjoyed the title King of Italy since birth].

Queen Victoria and Prince Albert

Princess Alexandrina Victoria of Kent was born on 24 May 1819 at Kensington Palace in London, the daughter of Princess Victoria of Saxe-Coburg-Saalfeld and Prince Edward, Duke of Kent and Strathearn (the fourth son of King George III). Sadly, the Duke died while she was still a baby and by the time her uncle, William IV, passed away in 1837, Victoria – she rejected Alexandrina for her regnal name – was next in line to wear the crown.

Victoria's childhood was shielded in the extreme. She was schooled at home and her mother tightly regulated her daily routine, this stifling maternal influence causing much stress between the two Victorias in the years to come. Yet, however much the mother tried to control her daughter's life, Victoria developed a strong will and keen interest in the world around her.

Victoria's desire for independence manifested itself in her attitude to affairs of the heart. Throughout her teenage years, the greatest object of her affection was her beloved spaniel,

Dash. But as she reached maturity, the question arose of who might make a suitable husband for the prospective monarch. Her uncle, the king, had his eye on a betrothal to Prince Alexander of the Netherlands, son of the Prince of Orange. But another uncle on her mother's side, Belgium's King Leopold, on whom the young Victoria doted, had other ideas. He preferred a match with his nephew, Prince Albert of Saxe-Coburg and Gotha. That Victoria and Albert were first cousins was not considered an impediment to their union.

Leopold arranged for Albert to visit Victoria in England in 1837, when she was just seventeen years of age. Albert bowled her over with his good looks and charming company and, although she was not prepared to commit to marriage immediately, it was clear that this would be the eventual likely outcome. So it was that she proposed to him in October 1839, and they were married in the Chapel Royal of St James's Palace on 10 February 1840. Of her wedding night, Victoria wrote in her journal: ' ... his excessive love and affection gave me feelings of heavenly love and happiness I never could have hoped to have felt before! He clasped me in his arms, and we kissed each other again and again! His beauty, his sweetness and gentleness – really how can I ever be thankful enough to have such a Husband! ... Oh! This was the happiest day of my life!'

Their life together was not without its challenges. For Albert, he had to establish exactly what his duties should encompass while his wife held the most preeminent position in the country. The British public were initially wary of this little-known prince from a moderately obscure foreign realm, while the nation's political class advised against making him a 'king consort' – a title he would never have conferred upon him, with even the lesser designation of 'prince consort' only coming four years before his death. As he himself noted, he was the husband in the household but not the master. However, over time, he established himself as Victoria's key advisor (a role previously held by the prime minister, Lord Melbourne). His opinions on matters political, economic, military and diplomatic came to hold great sway not only with his wife, but also with other prominent public figures in the country. He also contributed much to the nation's cultural life, from establishing Christmas traditions he brought over from Germany to playing a pivotal part in the Great Exhibition of 1851 and the subsequent regeneration of the London borough of South Kensington.

The couple would have nine children in total. Unsurprisingly in such an intense domestic set-up, there were occasional quarrels. Once, in the early 1850s, for instance, Albert wrote a tetchy letter to Victoria in which he complained about her 'hysterics' over a 'miserable trifle'. Yet most of the time they appeared to get along remarkably well. Doubtless, the various travails they faced brought them closer together. There were, for example, at least eight attempts made on the queen's life. Following an outpouring of public concern after one of the attacks, she was moved to comment that it was 'worth being shot at – to see how much one is loved'.

The antics of their eldest son, Albert Edward, Prince of Wales, were another cause of mutual concern. In late 1861, rumours abounded about the young prince's dalliance with an actress in Ireland. Albert was so perturbed that he made a visit to his son in Cambridge to warn him off such behaviour. It had already been a busy year, with Albert undertaking many official duties on behalf of Victoria, and it all proved too much. That December he fell ill with typhoid fever, dying on the 14 December. Victoria was overcome with grief, wearing black for most of the rest of her days and retreating from public life to such an extent that her invisibility to her subjects severely dented her popularity and led some to ask if the monarchy might even be under threat as a result.

Nonetheless, the country prospered as never before during her reign, which would break records for its longevity. Far from weakening the monarchy as an institution, it came to seem more robust than ever. While her love for Albert is unquestionable, her close friendship with a Scottish manservant, John Brown, after her husband's death did raise some eyebrows. Indeed, when Victoria herself died in 1901 at the age of eighty, she was buried with mementos of Albert but also a lock of Brown's hair. Yet, there can be little doubt

– as the following missives attest – that Albert was truly her *grande passion* and she his.

The Letters

Victoria was a prodigious writer and keeper of journals. The letters, diaries and memos she wrote over her lifetime have bequeathed us a record millions of words in length. As a result, the material that follows includes not only correspondence between Victoria and Albert, but also with King Leopold (these effectively being the first of her 'love letters' about Albert and, in the case of the very first item of correspondence, a 'non-love letter' warning against too great expectations). And, to finish, an entry from her diary gives some notion of the depth of love she carried for her husband until the end of his life. After her initial hesitation about Albert's visit to her in 1839, her words illustrate how quickly she fell for him. Yet the letters to Albert also point to a young woman intent on fulfilling her duties as monarch too. While she adored him, she recognised that in public life she was queen and thus the senior partner (see letters 7, 9, 10 and 11). Ultimately, though, she recognised that each was vital to the other in their partnership and that, personally, they completed one another.

Letter 1:

Victoria to King Leopold of Belgium (15 July 1839)

Buckingham Palace

My Dear Uncle,

... I shall send this letter by a courier, as I am anxious to put several questions to you, and to mention some feelings of mine upon the subject of my cousins' visit, which I am desirous should not transpire. First of all, I wish to know if Albert is aware of the wish of his father and you relative to me? Secondly, if he knows there is no engagement between us? I am anxious that you should acquaint Uncle Ernest [Prince Albert's father], that if I should like Albert, that I can make no final promise this year, for, at the very earliest, any such event could not take place till two or three years hence. For, independent of my youth, and my great repugnance to change my present position, there is no anxiety evinced in this country for such an event, and it would be more prudent, in my opinion, to wait till some such demonstration is shown – else if it were hurried it might produce discontent.

Though all the reports of Albert are favourable, and though I have little doubt I shall like him, still one can never answer beforehand for feelings, and I may not have the feeling for him that is requisite to ensure happiness. I may like him as a friend, and as a cousin, and as a brother, but not more; and should this be the case (which is not likely), I am very anxious that it should be understood that I am not guilty of any breach of promise, for I never gave any. I am sure you will understand my anxiety, for I should otherwise, were this not completely understood, be in a very painful position. As it is, I am rather nervous about the visit, for the subject I allude to is not an agreeable one to me. I have little else to say, dear Uncle, as I have now spoken openly to you, which I was very, very anxious to do ... ever your devoted niece, Victoria R.

Letter 2:

Victoria to King Leopold of Belgium (12 October 1839)

Windsor Castle

My Dear Uncle,

... The dear cousins arrived at half-past seven on Thursday, after a very bad and almost dangerous passage, but looking both very well, and much improved. Having no clothes, they could not appear at dinner, but nevertheless débuted after dinner in their négligé. Ernest is grown quite handsome; Albert's beauty is most striking, and he so amiable and unaffected – in short, very fascinating; he is excessively admired here ... We rode out yesterday and danced after dinner. The young men are very amiable, delightful companions, and I am very happy to have them here; they are playing some symphonies of Haydn under me at this very moment; they are passionately fond of music ...

Ever, my dearest Uncle, your devoted niece, Victoria R.

Letter 3:

**Victoria to King Leopold of Belgium (15 October 1839;
date of Victoria and Albert's engagement)**

Windsor Castle

My Dearest Uncle – This letter will, I am sure, give you
pleasure, for you have always shown and taken so an interest
in all that concerns me. My mind is quite made up – and
I told Albert this morning of it; the warm affection he
showed me on learning this gave me great pleasure. He seems
perfection, and I think that I have the prospect of very great
happiness before me. I love him more than I can say, and I
shall do everything in my power to render the sacrifice he
has made (for a sacrifice in my opinion it is) as small as I can.
He seems to have a very great tact – a very necessary thing in
his position. These last few days have passed like a dream to
me, and I am so much bewildered by it all that I hardly know
how to write; but I do feel very, very happy.

It is absolutely necessary that this determination of
mine should be known to no one but yourself, and Uncle
Ernest – till the meeting of Parliament – as it would be
considered otherwise neglectful on my part not to have
assembled Parliament at once to have informed them of it
.... Lord Melbourne, whom I of course have consulted about
the whole affair, quite approves my choice, and expresses
great satisfaction at the event, which he thinks in every way
highly desirable. Lord Melbourne has acted in this business,

as he has always done towards me, with the greatest kindness and affection.

We also think it better, and Albert quite approves of it, that we should be married very soon after Parliament meets, about the beginning of February; and indeed, loving Albert as I do, I cannot wish it should be delayed.

My feelings are a little changed, I must say, since last spring, when I said I couldn't think of marrying for three or four years; but seeing Albert has changed all this ...

Ever, dearest Uncle, your devoted niece, Victoria R.

Letter 4:
Albert to Victoria (15 October 1839)

My dearest, most beloved Victoria,

I am so touched by the evidence of trust that you give me in sending your letters, and by the so affectionate sentiments that you express towards me therein, that I scarcely know how to reply to you. How have I earned so much love and so much warm-hearted kindness? I am still unable to accustom myself to the truth of all that I see and hear, and can only believe that Heaven has sent down an angel to me, whose radiance is intended to brighten my life. May I succeed in making you quite, quite happy, as happy as you deserve to be!

With body and soul I remain for ever your slave.

Your devoted Albert

Letter 5:

Victoria to King Leopold of Belgium (29 October 1839)

Windsor Castle

My Dearest Uncle – Your most kind and most welcome letter of the 24th arrived yesterday, and gave me very, very great pleasure. I was sure you would be satisfied and pleased with our proceedings.

... Oh! dear Uncle, I do feel so happy! I do so adore Albert! He is quite an angel, and so very, very kind to me and seems so fond of me, which touches me much. I trust and hope I shall be able to make him as happy as he ought to be! I cannot bear to apart from him, for we spend such happy, delightful hours together.

... always, your most devoted niece and child, Victoria R.

Letter 6:

Albert to Victoria (15 November 1839)

Dearest, deeply loved Victoria,

According to your wish, and by the urging of my heart to talk to you and open my heart to you, I send these lines. We arrived safely at Calais ... The state of the tide and strong wind forced us to start at two-thirty in the morning, and we reached here at about six o'clock. Even then the *Firebrand* could not approach the quay, so that we decided to go ashore in a smaller boat. We both, Schenk, and all the servants were fearfully ill; I have hardly recovered yet. I need not tell you that since we left, all my thoughts have been with you at Windsor, and that your image fills my whole soul. Even in my dreams I never imagined that I should find so much love on Earth. How that moment shines for me when I was close to you, but with your hand in mine! Those days flew by so quickly, but our separation will fly equally so. Ernest wishes me to say a thousand nice things to you. With promises of unchanging love and devotion, your ever true Albert.

Letter 7:

Victoria to Albert (21 November 1839)

Buckingham Palace

... It is desired here that the matter [the announcement of the engagement] should be declared at Coburg as soon as possible, and immediately after that I shall send you the Order [of the Garter].

Your rank will be settled just before you come over, as also your rank in the army. Everything will be very easily arranged. Lord Melbourne showed me yesterday the Declaration, which is very simple and nice. I will send it you as soon as possible ...

Letter 8:

Victoria to Albert (28 November 1839)

This morning I received your dear, dear letter of the 21st. How happy do you make me with your love! Oh! My Angel

Albert, I am quite enchanted with it! I do not deserve such love! Never, never did I think I could be loved so much.

Letter 9:

Victoria to Albert (8 December 1839)

Windsor Castle

... As to your wish about your gentlemen, I must tell you quite honestly that it will not do. [Albert wished for greater say-so as to whom would be appointed as his household servants.] You may entirely rely upon me that the people who will be about you will be absolutely pleasant people, of high standing and good character. These gentlemen will not be in continual attendance on you; only on great occasions, and to accompany you when you go anywhere, and to dinners, etc. Seymour is your confidential attendant, and also Schenk and Anson, whom Lehzen (Victoria's companion and former governess) has written to you about. Old Sir George Anson has been told of your gracious wish to have him as Groom of the Bedchamber and is delighted.

I can only have lords, and they will not be peers, but lords, the eldest sons of dukes or marquesses, or earls (counts), and who as far as possible are not in Parliament, for then they need not change, but your people are appointed by you and not by me (nominally), and therefore, unless they were to vote against my government (which would be awkward), they need not change. You may rely upon my care that you shall have proper people and not idle and not too young, and Lord Melbourne has already mentioned several to me who would be very suitable ...

I have received today an ungracious letter from Uncle Leopold. He appears to me to be nettled because I no longer ask for his advice, but dear Uncle is given to believe that he must rule the roost everywhere ...

(continued 9 December)

Today I have had a council, and then I knighted the Mayor of Newport (who distinguished himself so much in that riot of the Chartists); he is a very timid, modest man, and was very happy when I told him orally how exceedingly satisifed I am with his conduct ... The officers have been rewarded too ... I am plaguing you already with tiresome politics, but you will in that find a proof of my love, because I must share with you everything that rejoices me, everything that vexes or grieves me, and I am certain you will take your part in it ...

Letter 10:

Victoria to Albert (26 December 1839)

Windsor Castle

... *The Historical Sketch* has interested us greatly; Lord Melbourne read it through immediately, I greatly thank you also for the genealogical tree you sent me.

Now, my dearest, to be about what is not so pleasant or amusing, I mean, now for business. I always think it safer to

write that in English, as I can explain myself better and
I hope you can read my English, as I try to be very legible.
I am much grieved that you feel disappointed about my
wish respecting your gentlemen, but very glad that you
consent to it, and that you feel confidence in my choice.
Respecting the treasurer, my dearest Albert, I have already
written at great length in my last letter, so I will not say
much about it today, but I will just observe that, tho' I fully
understand (indeed no one could feel more for you in the
very trying position you will be placed in than I do) your
feelings, it is absolutely necessary that an Englishman should
be at the head of your affairs; therefore (tho' I will not force
Mr Anson on you) I ask if it is not better to take a man in
whom I have confidence, and whom I know well enough to
trust perfectly, than a man who is quite a stranger, and whom
I know nothing of? ...

Letter 11:

Victoria to Albert (1 January 1840)

Buckingham Palace

... You have written to me in one of your letters about
our stay at Windsor but, dear Albert, you have not at all
understood the matter. You forget, my dearest love, that I
am the sovereign, and that business can stop and wait for
nothing. Parliament is sitting, and something occurs almost
every day, for which I may be required, and it is quite

impossible for me to be absent from London; therefore two or three days is already a long time to be absent. I am never easy a moment, if I am not on the spot, and see and hear what is going on, and everybody, including all my aunts (who are very knowing in all these things), says I must come out after the second day, for, as I must be surrounded by my court, I cannot keep alone. This is also my own wish in every way.

Now as to the arms: as an English prince you have no right, and Uncle Leopold had no right to quarter the English arms, but the sovereign has the power to allow it by Royal Command: this was done for Uncle Leopold by the Prince Regent, and I will do it again for you. But it can only be done by Royal Command. I will, therefore, without delay, have a seal engraved for you.

Farewell, dearest Albert, and think often of thy faithful Victoria R.

Letter 12:

Victoria to Albert (10 February 1840; their wedding day)

Dearest – How are you today, and have you slept well? I have rested very well, and feel very comfortable today. What weather! I believe, however, the rain will cease.

Send one word when you, my most dearly loved bridegroom, will be ready. Thy ever-faithful,

Victoria R.

Victoria's diary entry following Albert's death

(14 December 1861)

Went over at seven as I usually did. It was a bright morning;
the sun just rising and shining brightly ... Never can I forget
how beautiful my darling looked lying there with his face
lit up by the rising sun, his eyes unusually bright gazing as
it were on unseen objects and not taking notice of me ...
Sir James [Clark; royal physician] was very hopeful, so was
Jenner [William Jenner, another physician], and said it was a
'decided rally', but that they were all 'very, very, anxious' ... I
asked if I might go out for a breath of fresh air. The doctors
answered 'Yes, just close by, for half an hour!' I went out on
the terrace with Alice [her daughter]. The military band was
playing at a distance and I burst out crying and came home
again. Sir James was very hopeful; he had seen much worse
cases. But the breathing was the alarming thing – so rapid,
I think sixty respirations in a minute ... I bent over him and
said to him '*Es ist kleines Fräuchen*' (it is your little wife) and
he bowed his head; I asked him if he would give me *ein Kuss*
(a kiss) and he did so. He seemed half dozing, quite quiet ...
I left the room for a moment and sat down on the floor in
utter despair. Attempts at consolation from others only made
me worse. Alice told me to come in ... and I took his dear left
hand, which was already cold, though the breathing was quite
gentle and I knelt down by him ... Alice was on the other
side, Bertie [the Prince of Wales] and Lenchen [nickname of

Victoria and Albert's daughter, Helena] kneeling at the foot of the bed ... Two or three long but perfectly gentle breaths were drawn, the hand clasping mine and ... all, all, was over ... I stood up, kissed his dear heavenly forehead and called out in a bitter and agonising cry, 'Oh! My dear Darling!'

Edward VIII and Wallis Simpson

Edward Albert Christian George Andrew Patrick David Saxe-Coburg-Gotha was born at White Lodge, Richmond, on 23 June 1894, the son of Mary of Teck and Prince George (the Duke and Duchess of York). His great-grandmother was Queen Victoria and, in 1910, his father ascended to the throne as George V. In the same year, the teenaged Edward (who was known to family and friends as David) was made Prince of Wales, having become heir to the throne.

Edward soon proved a maverick among the royals. Good-looking and charismatic, he was a rule breaker who had little time for many of what he regarded as the stuffy traditions of his family. He travelled widely on behalf of his father in the 1920s and 30s, cutting a dash as talk of his fashion sense and the sagas of his private life filled the pages of the newspapers. Edward seemed purpose-made for the age of the pretty young things.

From early on, his father, the king, harboured concerns about where his son's romantic shenanigans would end. The prince had joined the Grenadier Guards in 1914 and was often to be found in France as the First World War rolled on. While on leave in Paris in 1917, he met one of his more exotic paramours, Marguerite Alibert, with whom he embarked on a passionate year-long affair. Six years later, Alibert would be acquitted of murder at the Old Bailey after shooting dead her husband in the Savoy Hotel on London's Strand. That Edward kept such company was a grave concern to those closest to him.

Falling in love with other men's wives became a theme of the prince's life. After Alibert, there was Winifred May Birkin, who became better known as Freda Dudley Ward after marrying a Liberal MP, William Dudley Ward, in 1913. Edward and Freda conducted an affair that lasted well into the 1930s, by which time she had divorced. Edward sent her several hundred letters over this period, though there is little evidence that he ever had any serious intention of taking her as his wife, even if he occasionally played with the idea. He was nonetheless deeply attached to her, so much so that Winston Churchill once described his love for her as 'obvious and undisguisable', not to mention 'pathetic'.

Yet in truth, Freda was but one of many lovers that the prince took. Another was Thelma Furness, who became a viscountess on her second marriage, to Marmaduke Furness, in 1926. It was in the same year that she first met

Edward, but it was not until 1930 that their relationship intensified. She, in turn, fatefully introduced the prince to Wallis Simpson a year later, with Edward and Wallis becoming lovers when Thelma was away in New York in early 1934. As Edward came to recognise Wallis as the great love of his life, he put distance between himself and both Freda and Thelma.

For the royal family at large, Wallis was the very last person that Edward ought to have fallen in love with. Variously counting against her was the fact that she was not herself titled, that she came from America, that she was already married and that the marriage was her second. Having divorced her first husband, a US naval officer called Winfield Spencer, she married an American-born shipping broker, Ernest Simpson, in 1928. While there were rumours that Edward was not her only extra-marital partner, the relationship between Wallis and the prince was so intense that it brought about one of the most dramatic constitutional dramas of the century – Edward VIII's abdication just a few months after he became king.

Not only was Wallis not to the taste of most of Edward's immediate family, but she posed an existential threat to the Crown. In a world much different to today, it was unimaginable for most of the country that an American divorcee might become queen. The government of Stanley Baldwin was adamantly opposed to any potential union, as was the

Archbishop of Canterbury, Cosmo Lang, who rejected the idea that Edward could carry on as head of the Church of England if he married her. Edward was left with three options, each of them in some way unpalatable. He might turn his back on the idea of marrying Wallis even once she had secured a divorce from Ernest; he could marry against the express advice of his government (which would in all probability have then resigned, causing a constitutional crisis of its own); or he could give up his claim to the throne. He chose the last option, formally abdicating on 10 December 1936. 'I have found it impossible,' he said in an address to the nation a day later, 'to carry the heavy burden of responsibility and to discharge my duties as king as I would wish to do without the help and support of the woman I love.'

His younger brother succeeded him as George VI. Wallis secured her divorce a few months later and she and the now Duke of Windsor were married at a private ceremony in France on 3 June 1937. There were no members of the royal family in attendance. As part of his abdication settlement, Edward received an allowance but was expected to live outside the country. Post-abdication, his apparent sympathy for Nazi Germany caused significant discomfort in Britain, and he spent most of the war as governor of the Bahamas, from where it was considered he would not be able to do much damage.

He never truly reconciled with his family, and relations with his mother in particular became ever more strained over the years. Edward and Wallis became globetrotting celebrities in the 1950s and 60s and spent much of their time when not travelling at home in France. A life-long heavy smoker, he developed throat cancer and died on 28 May 1972. His body was returned to England for burial by his family. Wallis passed away fourteen years later and was laid to rest alongside her husband.

The Letters

The letters between Edward and Wallis are fascinating not only as records of a love affair, but because they bear witness to a climactic series of events that threatened the very institution of the monarchy. While their relationship was not public knowledge until shortly before the abdication, it was well known in aristocratic circles. Exactly how much Wallis's husband Ernest knew of the nature of the relationship, and at what stage, is moot, although it is fair to say that he was aware of the affair for a significant period prior to their divorce. In the letters that follow, Edward often comes across in turns playful, doleful and temperamental. Wallis's letters are in some ways harder to dissect. At times she appears strong and practical, at other times sad and desperate, and we can sense that she suffered badly with cold feet as the possibility of abdication loomed. At other times, she appears selfless in her apparent desire to see Edward give her up for the sake of the throne. But whether she really believed Edward would throw her over, we can't be sure. Their missives do, though, give an insight into the thoughts, hopes and fears of two people caught in the eye of a historic storm. (Note that the pair used a lovers' code in their letters. They frequently refer to 'WE' in capitals, denoting 'we' by combining their initials (Wallis and Edward). They also regularly use the term 'eanum' to mean 'little', 'poor' etc.)

Letter 1:
Edward to Wallis (undated, 1935; Edward's first known letter to his lover)

St Austell Bay Hotel, Par, Cornwall

My Eanum – My Wallis

This is not the kind of Easter WE want but it will be all right next year. The Easter Bunny has brought this [unidentified present] from US all and Slipper [a cairn terrier that the prince had gifted Wallis the previous Christmas] says he likes it too, but it has to be fitted & christened later. I love you more and more and more each and every minute and miss you so terribly here. You do too, don't you my sweetheart? God bless WE. Always your David

Letter 2:

Edward to Wallis (23 July 1935)

HMS *Faulknor*

Tuesday, one o'clock a.m.

Wallis – A boy is holding a girl so very tight in his arms
tonight. He will miss her more tomorrow because he will
have been away from her some hours longer and cannot see
her till Wednesday night. A girl knows that not anybody or
anything can separate WE – not even the stars – and that
WE belong to each other for ever. WE love each other more
than life so God bless WE. Your David

Letter 3:

Wallis to Edward (August 1935)

Le Roc [a villa on the French Riviera]

I think it would be nice to have the [Winston] Churchill
drinks on the porch outside the drawing room. I also think
you are a very nice boy.

Letter 4:

Edward to Wallis (August 1935)

The Fort [Fort Belvedere in Surrey]

3 a.m.

Oh! A boy does miss and want a girl here so terribly tonight.
Will try and sleep now but am not hopeful yet. Have been
numbering our pictures. Please, please Wallis don't get

scared or lose faith when you are away from me. I love you more every minute and no difficulties or complications can possibly prevent our ultimate happiness. WE are so strong together in our purpose, which is our very life that it must not, cannot fail for any reason or obstacle that may confront us. I am sending this up to you in the morning with all the things I want to do and say to you right now. I do hate and loathe the present situation until I can start in to talk more than you do my sweetheart and am just going mad at the mere thought (let alone knowing) that you are alone there with Ernest. God bless WE for ever my Wallis.

You know your David will love you and look after you so long as he has breath in his eanum body.

Letter 5:
Edward to Wallis (Autumn 1935)
The Fort,
Saturday
Good morning my sweetheart in case I haven't been able to telephone. It's very sad we won't be here this weekend and Slipper is sad too. I've not told him about his cake yet. Take care of yourself until we meet at 'the Castle' this evening. More and more and more sweetheart and please miss me. God bless WE. David

Letter 6:

Edward to Wallis (26 December 1935)

Sandringham, Norfolk

Boxing Day!

Good night and good morning my sweetheart – as I won't
be able to say either by phone. It's helped so much getting a
few minutes talk alone at last this evening. I couldn't believe
it was possible to miss this way but it's so lovely although hell
while it lasts. It really is terrible here and so much the worst
Xmas I've ever had to spend with the family, far worse than
last year and that was bad enough. I just can't wait till seeing
you Monday [30 December] and to know that boat has sailed
for Canada [Ernest was set to travel abroad for business]. I'm
longing for an eanum letter Wallis. This one has to be eanum
as the mail is in a few minutes.

Letter 7:

Edward to Wallis (1 January 1936)

Good morning my sweetheart, Thank God last night is over
and let's go quickly this afternoon. Your lovely New Year
message helped a boy a lot in his lonely drowsy [sleep] and
he was feeling sad. Give Mary an eanum note for me to keep
until WE can be alone together again. Oh! My Wallis I know
we'll have *viel Glück* [good luck] to make us one this year. God
bless WE. Your David

Letter 8:

Edward to Wallis (April 1936)

Himley Hall [Dudley, Worcestershire]

THEY say that THEY liked this bracelet and that THEY want you to wear it always in the evening ... A boy loves a girl more and more and more.

Letter 9:

Edward to Wallis (5 June 1936)

The Fort

Friday night

Oh, my sweetheart it is so sad to return here without you. Hurry back quickly please and I know you will, as you must feel how much you are wanted and missed back here. You have been away far too long and you mustn't ever go away again. WE have just had a lovely long talk but that is a poor substitute for holding tight and making drowsy. No and not making own drowsies either as we have had to do far too often lately. Oh, make your return come quickly as I know you want it to.

My talk with Ernest was difficult this evening but I must get after him now or he won't move. [By now, Ernest and Wallis were heading for inevitable divorce, with Ernest seemingly conducting an extra-marital affair of his own with one of Wallis's closest friends.] It's so unsatisfactory until it's all settled and WE really are one and I can't bear your having to hear unpleasant things said as I'm just as sensitive as you

are, you know that. I know you will approve of Allen's plan
[Allen was the prince's lawyer and provided advice on the
easiest way of obtaining a divorce] but of course won't do a
thing until WE can discuss it. It's the only way. I must make
own drowsy. I expect you are doing too and I only hope a girl
is missing a boy as much as he is missing her. I'll finish in the
morning. God bless WE.

*On the 16th September came a startling apparent change
of mind from Wallis. They obviously discussed the matter
on the phone that day, too, but Edward seems determined
not to accept that the volte-face is genuine. Indeed, it would
prove not to be.*

Letter 10:
Wallis to Edward (16 September 1936)
Hotel Maurice, Rue de Rivoli, Paris
Wednesday night
Dear David,

It is too stupid to have to have a cold at just this moment.
However here I am tucked up in bed feeling very, very rotten.
But I did have a trout and two ears of delicious corn. This is
a difficult letter to write – but I feel it is easier than talking
and less painful. I must really return to Ernest for a great
many reasons, which please be patient and read. The first
being because we are so awfully congenial and understand

getting on together very well – which is really an art in marriage. We have no small irritations one for the other. I have confidence in his being able to take care of me and of himself. In other words, I feel secure with him and am only left with my side of the show to run. We each do our little jobs separately – with occasional help one for the other and it all runs smoothly no nerve strain. True we are poor and unable to do the attractive amusing things in life, which I must confess I do love and enjoy – also the possession of beautiful things is thrilling to me and much appreciated but weighed against a calm congenial life I choose the latter for I know that though I shall suffer greatly now I shall be a happier calmer old lady. I have been here alone tonight but seen my friends etc. I should rather have my husband than mere friends. No one can fill that place and no one can care (unless one has a family) so much. I know Ernest and have the deepest affection and respect for him. I feel I am better with him than with you – and so you must understand. I am sure dear David that in a few months your life will run again as it did before and without my nagging. Also you have been independent of affection all your life. We have had lovely beautiful times together and I thank God for them and know that you will go on with your job doing it better and in a more dignified manner each year. That would please me so. I am sure you and I would only create disaster together. I shall always read all about you – believing only half! – and you will know I want you to be happy. I feel sure I can't make you so and I honestly don't think you can me. I shall have Allen arrange the return of everything. I am sure that after this letter you will realise that no human being could assume this responsibility and it would be most unfair to make things harder for me by seeing me. Good-bye WE all say.

Wallis

Letter 11:

Edward to Wallis (16 September 1936)

The Fort

Twelve-thirty a.m.

Good night my Wallis. Why do you say such hard things to David on the telephone sometimes? Hard things like you would prefer to have someone else with you tonight when you are sick, that I would be bored, that I don't understand you and lots of others, which hurt me so and show that lack of faith and confidence in me, which makes me so terribly unhappy.

I'm so sad tonight sweetheart for this and other reasons. First of all that you feel so ill and that I'm not there to look after you. Then, that I won't see you before I go to Balmoral and not knowing when you will join me there. Oh! Please make it quickly my darling because every moment we are separated is a sad and lonely one.

I'm not going to worry you or ask you make plans when you don't feel in the health or the mood and the great thing is for you to get well again as quickly as possible. Our lovely holiday did do you good and now that's all undone. It makes me sick too. You see I do love you so entirely and in every way Wallis. Madly tenderly adoringly and with admiration and such confidence.

I feel like bursting tonight with love and such a longing to hold you tighter than I ever have before. Mr Loo [nickname for Slipper on account of his unfortunate toileting habits] and I are up here in our blue room and missing you like the dickens. It's hell but it's lovely in a way too. Please try and trust me like you love me and don't have any doubts. I promise you there is not the slightest reason to. If only you could read into my lightening brain you wouldn't. SHE doesn't doubt HIM (hand is hiding face) so don't you doubt me.

I'm exhausted now and will try to make drowsel, which I hope you will be able to do and I'll finish in the morning to send by airmail so as you can read all I have to say as quickly as possible. God bless WE

By October, Wallis was evidently still cautious about the future, but prepared to proceed with the divorce with Edward's support.

Letter 12:

Wallis to Edward (14 October 1936)

[On Claridge's writing paper, but sent from Felixstowe]

Thursday

My dear – This is really more than you or I bargained
for – this being haunted by the press. Do you feel you still
want me to go ahead as I feel it will hurt your popularity in
the country. Last night I heard so much from the Hunters
[friends] that made me shiver – and I am very upset and
ill today from talking until four. It nearly ended in a row,
as naturally it wasn't pleasant things I heard of the way the
man in the street regards me. I hear you have been hissed
in the cinema, that a man in a white tie refused to get up in
the theatre when they played *God Save the King* and that in one
place they added 'and Mrs Simpson'. Really David darling,
if I hurt you to this extent isn't it best for me to steal quietly
away. Today Ernest called up to say he was deluged with
cables from the US press and also that it had been broadcast
in America last night ... We can never stop America but I
hope we can get small announcements after it is over from
Beaverbrook [Lord Beaverbrook, the preeminent media
mogul of the period], which will be your Friday's job should
we decide to go ahead. I can't help but feel you will have
trouble in the House of Commons etc and may be forced to
go. I can't put you in that position. Also I'm terrified that
this judge here will lose his nerve – and then what? I am

sorry to bother you my darling – but I feel like an animal in a trap and these two buzzards working me up over the way you are losing your popularity through me. Do please say what you think best for all concerned when you call me after reading this. Together I suppose we are strong enough to face this mean world – but separated I feel eanum and scared for you, your safety etc. Also the Hunters say I might easily have a brick thrown at my car. Hold me tight please David.

By November, Edward was conjuring with the notion of laying out his dilemma to the British public and then retreating from public life for a few months while public opinion found its consensus. Wallis, though, was still giving him licence to cast her adrift for the sake of the Crown.

Letter 13:

Wallis to Edward (undated; written on Fort notepaper while she was on the way to France to avoid media attention)

Be calm with B [Prime Minister Stanley Baldwin] but tell the country tomorrow I am lost to you but Perry [Perry Brownlow, equerry to the prince who encouraged Wallis to dismiss the idea of marriage into the royal family] and myself can discreetly manage. We will let Bateman [royal telephone operator] know. A big big oo'oh [another term of affection used by the couple].

Letter 14:

Wallis to Edward (6 December 1936)

Lou Viei, Cannes

Sunday

Darling – I am sending this by air, as I think it important you have it before. I am so anxious for you not to abdicate and I think the fact that you do is going to put me in the wrong light to the entire world because they will say that I could have prevented it. Chips [Channon, Conservative MP with strong society links] has telephoned that the Cabinet have decided to force an answer by five today so I am sending this by air. If you will just give Baldwin my plan. If he turns it down then you have yours and the world could know a second compromise was turned down. My plan in detail is that you would say I [i.e. Edward] shall stand back of everything I have said [his offer to abdicate] (this saves you and me in the eyes of the world because naturally if you did not make this clear you would be a cad in the eyes of the world and I would be the woman well you know that was turned down – so that sentence printed in every newspaper saves that) to go on with the main theme – I will repeat again what to say to Mr B. I stand back of everything I have said but I do not wish to create a situation within the country so I therefore will not press the issue at the moment but reopen it in the autumn. Then if in the autumn they turn it down, your plan comes into action. I ask you to put that to Mr B. so that no one can say we haven't tried in every way to do our duty in such a big cause. Personally, I think he will turn it down and then we have the glorious other but surely if it should go we will make the sacrifice of not seeing each other for that length of time. In fact we can arrange to secretly through our friends. I feel so terrified of what the world will say and I again repeat that they will say I could have stopped it. Also I don't see how anyone has the power to push the decree forward so be very careful that people would not insinuate the one legal reason – also the money – and the right sort of name with HRH. Don't be carried away with the idea alone that things can happen for us so quickly – all those three things [that is to say, the abdication, her divorce and a suitable title and allowance for Edward] must be bound up impossible to find a flaw. My idea might go in Oct so it would appeal to the world. We would have made a gesture that is sporting fair. If B. turns it down in Oct – thare [sic] would be an uproar. No one but Baldwin and the dominions want you to go and as the Aga Khan telephoned they haven't given you a fighting. The people in the press are clamouring for a word from you. You owe it to them to tell them something and if you made that gesture by radio – by October Mr B. couldn't afford to say no and I think the Dominions could be won over. Think my sweetheart isn't it better in the long run not to be hasty or selfish but back up your people and make an eight-month sacrifice for them. Then they give you what you want and if they can't we will be vindicated in the eyes of the world and no one can say you shirked and ran away when the people were rallying to your aid. Mr Baldwin has misrepresented your case already in Parliament – by keeping repeating into their heads I must be queen. You must speak and tell the plan of the duchess and my plan [that neither Wallis nor any offspring would be entitled to Edward's royal titles or privileges]. Don't be silenced and leave under cloud I beseech you and in abdication no matter in what form unless you can let the public know that the Cabinet has virtually kicked you out by repressing two proposals. I can't support you unless you tell the country the two proposals. I must have any action of yours understood by the world but hidden by B. we would have no happiness and I think the world would turn against me. When now we have their sympathy. I worry too about the legal side because that would be a tragedy if they refused me [a divorce]. This plea is to beg you to submit my idea to B. If he refuses – I have spoken to you so there is no more to say except I'm holding you tighter than ever. Wallis

Letter 15:
Wallis to Edward (12 December 1936, the day after Edward's abdication speech to the nation)
Saturday
Darling – My heart is so full of love for you and the agony of not being able to see you after all you have been through

is pathetic. At the moment we have the whole world against us and our love – so we can't afford to move about very much and must simply sit and face these dreary months ahead and I think I shall have to stay here. It may be safer than moving and a house is more protection than a hotel from the press and the fanatics. I am thinking where is the best place for you because you must have people with you always. The Hunters would come out also Perry and Kitty [Brownlow], the Buists etc. A man called Bedaux – Americans – have offered their place to you. It is near Tours. The Rogers say it is lovely. Perhaps it is too near here. Then I hear Ralph Grimthorpe has offered you his house at Sorrento, Italy. I also hear that Lincoln Ellsworth has a lovely house in Switzerland that you could probably get – and in my opinion Mimizan is safe. I don't think you will be happy long at Enzesfeld and besides you couldn't stay forever. I think after Xmas the limit. Anyway we will find something for you darling and I am feeling all your feelings of loneliness and despair, which must face you on this new beginning. If we could have been together during the waiting it would have been so much easier. I long for you so. I hear that there is an organisation of women who have sworn to kill me. Evans is investigating. We must not take any risks because to have an accident come now would be too much to bear – so please be a 'sissy' about protection. I am. There is nothing I can begin to say about

Perry's friendship for us. It has been absolutely marvellous
in every way. Do tell him. I can't because I begin to cry. I
have never seen anything like it. I don't know your name
but rather hoped it would be Prince [sic] of Windsor. I
suppose we will have difficulty about a name for poor me
as York [sic]. I don't suppose will make me HRH [Her
Royal Highness]. Above all we want to have a dignified
position no matter where we are. That is also important to
the throne. Your broadcast was very good my angel and it is
all going to be so very lovely. Make ooh! It is cruel the laws
are such that we can't see each other until April. However
everything must be done to try and placate the legal side. I
can't believe the government would want more scandal and
everything raked up again at the time of the coronation.
Some of the papers – *Times, Telegraph* and *Morning Post* – have
been disloyal to you and foul to me. However it is all over
now. I hope you will never regret this sacrifice and that your
brother will prove to the world that we still have a position
and that you will be given some jobs to do. I am sending
Ladbrook [Edward's chauffeur] home as he wants to go
but he will come out to you anywhere and you must have a
car. I am engaging a local chauffeur. I think the detectives
hate the job but I must have them and if the Home Office
withdraws them I shall have to have two out and pay them.
Monckton or Allen [Edward's legal advisors] could select
them and I shall pay out of the savings account. It is worth

it God knows with all these threatening letters. I love you
David and am holding so tight.

Wallis

Hello everybody – and a pat to Slippy Poo.

Letter 16:
Edward to Wallis (1 January 1937)
Schloss Enzesfeld [Austria]

Hello! My sweetheart – Such a very happy New Year I wish
for WE from the fastness of my 'exile' – my exile from you
and not from England my darling and although it is still
a matter of weary months to wait it is lovely to have 1936
behind us and only this and many more happy years together
to look to. Oh! We will make it – but this separation but
'by golly' it is hard and a terrible strain. If it wasn't for that
unsatisfactory telephone then I really would go mad. Oh!
Poor everybody WE all say and HE is so scared of losing
his hair pin that he does want HER to hurry and send him
another to secure the old one. I'm giving this to Storrier
[Edward's Scotland Yard detective] to take to you tomorrow
evening along with an eanum New Year present (the two
feathers were for Christmas) in which you will find three
letters for you and some monograms to choose one from
for notepaper etc. Have a good talk with Storrier and then
he'll return to report the situation and you could give him a
letter for me if you have written one. I'll have to watch out

for our interests in England like the dickens although I have loyal friends like Walter [Monckton] and Ulick [Alexander, Keeper of the Privy Purse] and of course E. R. Peacock [a financial adviser to Edward] and [George] Allen. Oh! How hopeless writing is when WE have so much to say and arrange about the future. Maybe it would be better for Aunt Bessie [Wallis's beloved aunt and an important confidante] to return as there's not much for her to do and is of course a slight extra expense to the Rogers [old friends of Wallis, with whom Bessie was staying] ... I'm glad its quieter for you too now from the newspaper end but it will all boil up again in April damn it. Mr Loo sends a lot of dog kisses and I send a four-leaf clover. It's a cultivated plant but there were two on one root and I have kept and pressed the other. Oh, 'make ooh' to think you'll hold this piece of paper. God! How I love you love you my Wallis my beloved sweetheart more and more and more. I'm holding so tight all the time until that dear lovely precious day. Oh! God make it come quickly and bless WE this year and always. Your David

Wallis's letter below was written at a time when it was becoming apparent that Edward was set to become an outcast, his 'wretched brother', the king, firmly of the belief that Edward's conduct had been utterly disgraceful. A week previous to this letter, it should also be noted, Slipper had died after being bitten by a viper.

Letter 17:

Wallis to Edward (14 April 1937)

Wednesday

My darling ... I have thought up a marvellous thing to say
when you announce when our wedding will take place – this
I shall save to tell you about when you arrive. You must now
give your ammunition around a bit. I am so pleased with my
other eanum gun and both Rogers think it OK and grand.
WE don't care – but now we must protect WE and as we
have been turned adrift we have an excellent chance. How
stupid two camps. Well who cares let him [King George] be
pushed off the throne. The minute the family split – danger.
A fine history his will be after his behaviour to you. As you
know a series of horrid books about you are appearing in
England – and even the *Daily Mirror* has an editorial on how
well they were behaving about you – you will of course have
to write your side in self-defence. It is the most wicked
campaign and it must not succeed. I love you more than ever
my sweetheart. So much trouble WE have had together but
it only makes my love grow stronger for you my dear. Please
take care of yourself. I am always worrying in case something
should happen. Wallis

Letter 18:

Edward to Wallis (14 April 1937; his last letter to her before their marriage on 3 June)

Landhaus Appesbach [Austria]

Oh, my beloved one – What a month of socks this April is turning out to be. Never mind it will all be over soon and they can sock us all they want to when we are together because then we'll be able to sock back at them won't WE darling? Only they are eanum harder to take alone and the agony of drafting letters on the telephone ... This is just a line to say I love you more and more my own sweetheart and praying that the next eighteen days and nights wont drag too interminably for WE. Poor WE – and there must be such a huge big store of happiness for us after all of these months of hell ... It will be lovely looking for our eanum new home somewhere or maybe we'll be able to afford to build one. Oh, God I love you so Wallis so pleased that HE may bless WE. Please take care of your precious self for your David like he is doing for a girl because it's all he's got left in the world and it's all that he wants.

Selected Bibliography and Further Reading

Akrigg, G. P. V. (ed.), *Letters of King James VI & I* (University of California Press, 1984).

Aspinall, A. (ed.), *The Letters of King George IV, 1812–1830* (Cambridge University Press, 1938).

Benson, Arthur Christopher (ed.), *The Letters of Queen Victoria* (John Murray, 1908).

Bergeron, David M., *King James & Letters of Homoerotic Desire* (University of Iowa Press, 1999).

Black, Ladbroke (ed.), *The Love Letters of Henry the Eighth to Anne Boleyn* (Blandford Press, 1933).

Bloch, Michael (ed.), *Wallis and Edward: Letters 1931–1937: The Intimate Correspondence of the Duke and Duchess of Windsor* (Penguin, 1986).

Brewer, J. S., Brodie, R. H. and Gairdner, James (eds.), *Letters and Papers of the Reign of Henry VIII* (Kraus Reprint Co., 1965).

Bruce, John (ed.), *Charles I in 1646: Letters of King Charles the First to Queen Henrietta Maria* (Printed for the Camden Society, 1856).

Bruce, John (ed.), *Letters of Queen Elizabeth and King James VI of Scotland* (Printed for the Camden Society, 1849).

Bryant, Sir Arthur (ed.), *The Letters of King Charles II* (Cassell, 1968).

Campbell, Hugh (ed.), *The Love Letters of Mary Queen of Scots, to James Earl of Bothwell* (Longman, 1824).

Chatterton, E. Keble (ed.), *Royal Love Letters* (Mills & Boon, 1911).

Coxhead, J., *Royal Love Lyrics, From Royal Love Letters* (J. Coxhead, 1809).

Crawford, Anne, *Letters of the Queens of England, 1100–1547* (Sutton Publishing, 1994).

De La Ronciere, Charles, *Napoleon's Letters to Marie Louise* (Farrar & Rinehart, Inc. 1935).

Doebner, Dr Richard, *Memoirs of Mary, Queen of England* (Leipzig, Veit & Co., 1886).

Hall, Henry Foljambe (ed.), *Napoleon's Letters to Josephine, 1796–1812* (J. M. Dent and Co., 1901).

Jagow, Dr Kurt (ed.) and Dugdale, E. T. S. (trans.), *Letters of the Prince Consort, 1831–1861* (E. P. Dutton, 1938).

Johnstone, Hilda (ed.), *Letters of Edward, Prince of Wales, 1304–1305* (Roxburghe Club, 1931).

Letters between an illustrious personage and a lady of honour, at B******* (Logographic Press, 1785).

Litterfield, Walter (ed.) and Strachey, Lionel, *Love Letters of Famous Royalties and Commanders* (The John Mcbride Co., 1909).

Marcus, Leah S., Mueller, Janel and Rose, Mary Beth (eds.), *Elizabeth I: Collected Works* (University of Chicago Press, 2002).

Pritchard, R. E., *Scandalous Liaisons: Charles II and his Court* (Amberley Publishing, 2018).

Sanders, Margaret (ed.), *Intimate Letters of England's Queens* (Museum Press, 1957).

Smith, Douglas (ed. and trans.), *Love & Conquest: Personal Correspondence of Catherine the Great and Prince Grigory Potemkin* (Northern Illinois University Press, 2004).

The Royal Collection Trust (find online at www.rct.uk) is a trove of royal treasures and well worth an explore.